# The Essene Odyssey

Hugh J. Schonfield was born in London in 1901 and was educated at St Paul's School and the University of Glasgow. He specialized as a historian with particular reference to the Near East, but is probably best known for his researches into the origins of Christianity. He was the first Jew to make an objective and historical translation of the New Testament from the Greek into English; a work which received the highest praise for accuracy and realism from churchmen and scholars. He was also one of the scholars who worked on the Dead Sea Scrolls after their discovery in 1947. He wrote over thirty books, the most popular being *The Passover Plot*, which has sold over 3,000,000 copies worldwide.

Dr Schonfield was a President of the Commonwealth of World Citizens and of the International Arbitration League and was nominated for the Nobel Peace Prize in 1959 for his services towards international harmony. Hugh Schonfield died in 1988.

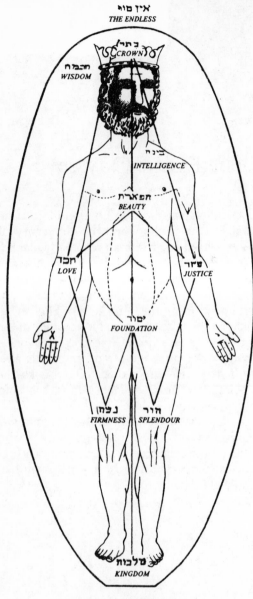

אין סוף
**THE ENDLESS**

חתר
CROWN

חכמה
WISDOM

בינה
INTELLIGENCE

תפארת
BEAUTY

חסד
LOVE

דין
JUSTICE

יסוד
FOUNDATION

נצח
FIRMNESS

הוד
SPLENDOUR

מלכות
KINGDOM

SKY MAN
The Expression of the Deity in Creation
through His Attributes.
From Ginsberg, *The Kabbalah*,
(Routledge & Kegan Paul, 1955)

# Hugh J. Schonfield

D S LITT FIAL

# The Essene Odyssey

*The Mystery of the True Teacher
and the Essene Impact on the Shaping
of Human Destiny*

# ELEMENT

Shaftesbury, Dorset ● Rockport, Massachusetts
Brisbane, Queensland

© Hugh Schonfield 1984

First published in Great Britain in 1984 by
Element Books Limited
Longmead, Shaftesbury, Dorset

Second impression 1985
Third impression 1993

Published in the USA in 1993 by
Element, Inc.
42 Broadway, Rockport, MA 01966

Published in Australia in 1993 by
Element Books Limited for
Jacaranda Wiley Limited
33 Park Road, Milton, Brisbane 4064

Cover illustration by Shane Feeney
Cover design by Max Fairbrother
Designed by Humphrey Stone
Printed and bound in Great Britain by
Dotesios Ltd, Trowbridge, Wiltshire

British Library Cataloguing in Publication
data available

Library of Congress Cataloging in Publication
data available

ISBN 0–906540–63–1

# Contents

"And one chief man shall come again from the sky . . . the best of the Hebrews . . ."

*The Sibylline Oracles*

## Introduction

# From Qumran to Kashmir

This work is concerned with the Messianic, an interpretation of the human story and world history as conceived by the ancient Hebrews and expounded by the mysterious sect of Essenes. It acquaints us first of all with the initiative in the second century before Jesus – a time of crisis for the Jews – of a remarkable yet anonymous sage known as the True Teacher or Teacher of Righteousness. It goes on to trace the consequences of his vision as interpreted by his followers and taken up by his claimed successors, in particular John the Baptist and Jesus of Nazareth. From here we pursue the spread of Essene ideology through various faiths in East and West and from century to century.

My book deals also with the intriguing question as to what relationship Jesus had had with the Essenes. Had they been his instructors and given him their assistance? And what of John the Baptist? Had he been an Essene? It did not call for much learning to discover links between the Essenes and primitive Christianity, though they are not mentioned by name in the New Testament. Fiction writers took up the challenge as well as students of religion, and unfortunately a great deal of bogus information about the Essenes got into print. This could only be corrected if access could be obtained to genuine first hand information.

What has been attempted in this book would thus not have been practicable a few years ago: we did not have sufficient access to this source material. It has been the progressive recovery over the past two centuries of a number of ancient documents, in whole or part, known and unknown, which has transformed the situation. The great break through into Essene territory seemed to come in the middle of the present century with the fortuitous and remarkable discovery at Qumran in Palestine of the manuscripts commonly known as the Dead Sea Scrolls. Here it would appear, were actual Hebrew documents some two thousand years old, written and used by the Essenes, and which might be capable of revealing much about them and disclosing many of their secrets. But it was not to be so easy and straightforward. The Brotherhood had guarded its secrets well by the employment of ciphers and cryptic language. Much did become clear, particularly about Essene government, organisation, and codes of behaviour. But on questions of dates and personalities there was much conflict of erudite opinion. To an appreciable extent this was due to religious viewpoints. We were in the dangerous area of immediately pre-Christian thinking which might affect our doctrinal positions. Since then there has also been the development of a more responsible and scientific approach to the comparison and assessment of such material. In addition, there has been a greater willingness for objective and relatively impartial comparison between historical records and the relics of different religions and cults. Dogmatism is still strong, but not so completely dominant.

It has only been practicable since the discovery of the Dead Sea Scrolls to apprehend not only the full character and influence of the Essene propaganda, but also its extent. At the commencement of the Christian era there was an outpouring of a strange literature, didactic and prophetic, much of it ascribed to the great biblical personalities. These dramatic and informative writings, many of which will be cited in the pages of this book are now academically classified as *Apocrypha* and *Pseudepigrapha* and are little known to the general reader. To experience them is indeed a revelation, and it can be imagined what their effect on Jewish attitudes was in the critical times in which they appeared. I recall with awe seeing the tables on which some of them were written and the very ink-wells the scribes used.

We have to allow now what was previously so clearly evident to no more than a relatively few scholars, that the Messianic concepts to which Jesus and others of his time were responsive were far from being confined to biblical sources. They were being shaped by writings and teachings emanating largely from the Essenes, and widely regarded as inspired. Until it became possible in recent times to be fully aware of this, and to have access to much of the literature, the true story of Christian beginnings could not be ascertained. Our perspectives were incorrect and almost inevitably so were our conclusions. The circumstances have not yet been apprehended by the vast majority of Christians.

Speaking for myself, my own interest in the Messianic – as a Jewish boy – began some seventy years ago, and I have pursued it step by step ever since. The way has been far from easy; and in

Jewish, and even more in Christian contexts, I have encountered an extraordinary, almost perverse, ignorance and lack of understanding. On the other hand there have been some distinguished Christian scholars who all along were ready to give me much guidance and assistance. What disposed me to my unusual pursuit I cannot tell. It sprang from an interior urge. There it was; and in the course of my quest I was to write a number of books, each of which contributed something more to my comprehension. Progressively I was accumulating a remarkable range of resources in languages ancient and modern which permitted a greater facility for comparison, and continually fresh literary finds added to my store. In this volume a substantial number of texts are quoted, many of which will be unfamiliar to the general reader; and at the worst its value will lie in having assembled them in a single work for his enlightenment. I should add that I have been closely involved with on-site archaeological investigation and specialised group discussion of evidences.

My desire, however, has always been to reach the layman – for it is his or her philosophy of life that counts. I have been all for the dictum of Jesus, "What you hear in the ear, that shout from the roof tops." From my point of view that applies no less to many of the tenets of an esoteric fraternity like the Essenes. There is knowledge, of course, which it would be harmful to entrust to unreliable people. But by and large most of us have a right to know what the existence of our planet and our being on it is about, in so far as propositions and insights can inform us.

There could be some psychic cause in the scheme of things why so much that is evidential was lost for centuries, and is now being restored to us when we are experiencing a period of transition and grave uncertainty. This has already been with us for some time, and seems likely to continue in the foreseeable future. At various epochs people have been obsessed by the feeling of the imminence of overwhelming catastrophe and have reacted accordingly. But with the destructive horrors which science has contrived, modern generations have had more reason than many previously to anticipate a final disaster. The curious fact is, however, that such periods have proved to be not ends but incentives to fresh achievements, impulsions to progress and fresh exciting adventures. We are drawn back in order to be propelled forward like an arrow from a bow. This is where the Essenes, and not only they, had some insight. They favoured the view that the human story would consist of a series of advances and setbacks. The process would have a termination so far as the Earth was concerned, when it had outlived its usefulness; but only so that it might continue in another and more extensive context.

It is perhaps because of this 'try, try, and try again' urge in our make-up that we encounter an extraordinary persistence of certain ideas in inhospitable surroundings and under the most adverse conditions. We find people ready to endure extremes of suffering for their convictions, and we also find beneath the surface an inter-locking of relationships between alien and even opposing creeds, so that there is – largely unacknowledged – much borrowing and cross-fertilization. This reflects a fundamental seeking after a common language of the spirit, which expresses and gives access to higher flights of conception. We may describe this as a quest for God; but essentially it is a quest for the perfect expression of our species, for the Ideal Man.

We are worshippers of God because it has been conceived that He created Man in His likeness, and we desire to be conformed to that likeness so that we may have access to all that He represents for us, to all time and space, to all that the teeming Universe has to offer. Our humanity is seen as a passport to immortality, for through it we mortals are made conscious of a participation in all that is, and was, and shall be. In microcosm we boldly assert our inherent relationship to the macrocosm. As children of God we have a built-in incentive to strive towards the stars.

With such matters as these the Essenes, like other mystics, were intimately concerned. But while they soared into the heights they kept their feet firmly on the ground. They knew that the world was a training ground. The battles had to be fought and the victory won here before we could be transferred elsewhere. The Kingdom of God had to be achieved, which meant "Thy will be done on earth, as it is in heaven." How short-sighted are our modern science-fiction writers, who can only think to transfer to the heavens all our worst qualities!

Delving into the manner in which Man's emancipation from evil should be accomplished, the Essenes developed the philosophy of the Messianic, a philosophy which was both spiritual and political. The one would be ineffective without the other. Whoever, therefore, might serve as an exemplar must also be seen in a regal capacity, not only in respect of chosen individuals, but also in respect of a chosen collectivity of individuals, the Elect.

Thus the Essenes built up from the Bible and other sources a dualistic interpretation both of the Messianic office, in one aspect priestly and in the other regal, and of the Elect, who would reign on earth as both kings and priests (*Rev.*v. 10). The priestly aspect would involve redemptive suffering and humiliation, while the regal would involve exemplary qualities of wisdom and organization. From these ideas there developed the doctrine of two Messiahs (anointed ones), of priestly stock and of regal stock. At the beginning of the Christian era, when the Last Times were believed by many to have commenced, the followers of John the Baptist identified him with the first, and the followers of Jesus the Nazorean identified him with the second. In the case of Jesus there came to be assigned to him the two rôles, that of the Priestly Sufferer in his first advent and potentially as the Davidic World Ruler in his expected second advent. Jewish speculation also embraced the concept of the two Messiahs, Messiah ben Joseph and Messiah ben David.

Bound up with these developments was the mystical concept of the Son of Man, which associated the universe with the human figure, the Sky Man, the archetypal primordial Man, the projection of the divine qualities and objectives in Creation, in whose likeness the first man, Adam, was fashioned (*Gen.*i.27).

In the background of such ideas we find the mysterious figure of the True Teacher, or Teacher of Righteousness, venerated by the Essenes and himself hailed as 'the Man', and also revered as Prophet, Priest and King (Lawgiver). What has never been cleared up, despite erudite attempts, is who the True Teacher actually was – assuming him to have been a person known to history – and when he lived. We have only really been conscious that he ever existed since the recent discovery of the Dead Sea Scrolls. The *Moreh-zedek* (Teacher of Righteousness) comes before us like the mysterious *Melchi-zedek* (King of Righteousness) in the *Epistle to the Hebrews,* "without father, without mother, without ancestry, having neither beginning of days nor end of life" (*Heb.*vii.3). The mystery about him has remained profound; a religious founder and father figure who has eluded positive identification thanks to the veneration which kept him incognito outside the ranks of the Brotherhood's initiates, and probably from many inside. Yet he has left a widespread impress, as this book will seek to show.

As a historian, specialising in Christian origins, I was challenged by this mystery from the first disclosure of its existence. In my experimental researches, published in 1956 under the title *Secrets of the Dead Sea Scrolls*, I had luckily been able to pick up some significant clues; but I had not appreciated at the time where they would lead me, and into what strange places. Subsequently I was to realize that in a great many of the books I had written there were other pointers, as was inevitable as I had been delving into relevant material.

The Teacher had emerged out of a developing conflict between a puritanical Hebraism and a hedonistic Hellenism. This had reached a climax in the second century B.C. through the persecuting policy of the Seleucid monarch, Antiochus Epiphanes, as a result of which the Temple of God at Jerusalem had been polluted and converted to the worship of Zeus Olympius. Nothing so horrifying as this had been experienced in the history of Israel, and nothing therefore more surely indicated to the Pious (the *Chasidim*) that the climax of the Ages was fast approaching. What made matters so much worse was that the corrupt chief priests were in league with the persecutors.

Near the end of the struggle, in which the Jewish Faith was defended in arms by the priestly Maccabees, a number of the Pious fled the country in order to be free to preserve the practice of their religion in purity. They found a refuge in the wilderness in the 'Land of Damascus', and were joined here by the True Teacher who brought yet more with him. He was to draw up for the exiles a strict code of Jewish behaviour, pledging them to a New Covenant in accordance with *Jer*.xxxi.31-37. The Teacher was to die in exile. But as the outcome of his initiative, and after many vicissitudes, the Brotherhood of the Essenes took shape. There was a return to Israel by many, especially during the reign of Herod the Great when it was believed that the climax of the Ages was imminent. Their principal centre for the next critical century was at Qumran close to the western shore of the Dead Sea. Here the massive work of copying and distributing prophetic and didactic literature was sustained until the settlement was overrun by the Romans in the war of 67-70 A.D.

This might seem to have signified the end of Essenism. But it was not so. There were other settlements in Syria, and also in Egypt where the Essenes were known as Therapeuts. The eccentric Jewish philosopher of the first century A.D., Philo of Alexandria, held them in high esteem. These offshoots of the parent body continued for some centuries, and much of their teaching and literature was carried far and wide, influencing religious and eclectic groups of many kinds, Jewish, Christian, and later Muslim, as we shall demonstrate.

It is with these developments that much of this book will be concerned. For the author it has been an exciting quest.

We shall also be delving into certain Essene mysteries preserved from their ancient beginnings, which were handed on through the centuries and became mingled with the traditions of other faiths. It has been no easy task to trace some of these relationships.

Indeed, the task would have proved quite impossible had I not found a key which not only disclosed one of the Essene secrets, but also opened up associations which had not before been apprehended.

It was characteristic of the Essenes, as professed masters of secret lore, that they employed attributes and disguises with reference to particular individuals and groups. This was to indicate that they were representative of qualities and forces, good and bad, as well as of actual people. Their character was reflected by the employment of suitable pseudonyms. Thus in the texts we encounter the True Teacher, the Wicked Priest, the Lion of Wrath, and so on. In effect they were rendered timeless.

But the Essenes also employed various types of codes and ciphers, largely for didactic and expository purposes, but sometimes as a safeguard to prevent disclosure of a vital secret. J.M. Allegro, who played an important part in deciphering the Dead Sea Scrolls and also in the opening of the copper scroll relating to the hiding places of Essene material treasures, speaks of this aspect.

An intriguing problem which has presented itself during the work has been the deciphering of a number of different secret codes in which several of the works were written ... to keep certain works especially secret. And in one case they contrive to write most but not all of the words backwards, and use a mixture of four or five alphabets, including one or two of their own invention.[1]

Of such ciphers it has long been known that some were employed in the Hebrew text of the Bible. One is prominent in the book of the Prophet Jeremiah, as I have illustrated in Part One chapter 11 of this work. Why it was introduced there we shall have reason to consider. It was a very simple cipher. There are twenty-two letters in the Hebrew alphabet. The cipher exchanged the first eleven letters for the last eleven in reverse order. With the English alphabet this would mean that Z was substituted for A, Y for B, X for C, and so on. In Hebrew this would be *Aleph*=*Tau*, *Bet*=*Shin*. The cipher was therefore known as *Atbash*.

While working on the Dead Sea Scrolls, not long after the find at

Qumran, I thought of applying the Atbash cipher to certain mysterious, indeed apparently meaningless, words, which immediately became intelligible. For example, in the book often called the *Damascus Document,* emanating from the Essenes, it was said that members had to be instructed in the *Book of Hago,* while judges had to be authorities on it. The word was clearly a disguise. But the Atbash code converted *Hago* (הגו) into *Tsoreph* (צרף), which signifies testing or proving. Reference was therefore being made to a work known as the *Book of Proving* or *Test Book,* which might be inferred to relate to guidance in the Essene methods of expounding and interpreting the Scriptures. The Jewish sectaries spoke much in other aspects of trial and testing. Indeed, before the advent of the Kingdom of God, they expected the Woes of Messiah, a period of suffering and persecution, when the forces of Evil would be let loose against the Saints (*Dan.xi.*35, xi. 10; *Rev.iii.* 10).

This was challenging. But something even more exciting was to follow. In a key sectarian book, the *Assumption* or *Testament of Moses,* dating, according to Canon Charles, somewhere around 9–30 A.D., there was a remarkable reference to instructions given by the Lawgiver (Moses) to his successor Joshua (Jesus): "Receive thou this writing that thou mayst know how to preserve the books which I shall deliver unto thee. And thou shalt set these in order and anoint them with oil of cedar, and put them away in earthern vessels in the place which He made from the beginning of the creation of the world, that His name shall be called upon until the day of Repentance in the visitation wherewith the Lord shall visit them in the consummation of the End of the Days (i. 16–17)."

Here we are told about secret books to be placed in sealed jars and hidden away until the Last Times, when they would be brought to light for the instruction of the faithful. One might have been reading about arrangements for hiding the secret writings of the Essenes, like the Dead Sea Scrolls, in sealed jars in caves!

But there was something more. In the same book there is reference to an individual, a man of the priestly tribe of Levi, who upheld the Mosaic Laws when the Syrian monarch Antiochus Epiphanes sought to abolish their observance. The date indicated is around 170–165 B.C. The man's name, clearly a contrived one, is given in the existing Latin text as TAXO, which in the original Hebrew would have been TACHO (תחו). The name was still unintelligible; but treating it as an instance of Atbash it yielded the well-known Hebrew personal name ASAPH ( אסף ). The identity of the man in the text had been further disguised by making him something of a composite character representative of the faithful in Israel. But the name disclosed would itself appear to have been a carefully selected pseudonym. This was to afford an important lead.

The most familiar Biblical possessor of the name Asaph had been a Levite in the time of King Solomon, reputed to have had a hand in the construction of the Temple at Jerusalem. Asaph's male descendants, with possibly other recruited Levites, became choristers in the Temple, called Sons of Asaph, and in the Hebrew Psalter twelve psalms are assigned to him (*Psalms* l and lxxiii-lxxxiii). Appropriately there was a collection of psalms among the Dead Sea Scrolls, and in a much earlier find of such documents there had been many more psalms. Those now recovered were largely autobiographical in character, commencing with the words "I thank Thee, O Lord." On this account it was being suggested by scholars that many of them might be compositions by the True Teacher of the Essenes, in which he had recorded something of his sufferings and deliverances.

The Biblical Asaph was to become a legendary figure in Jewish and Muslim literature, master of secret arts and medical skill. Even in a late book of the Bible he is called in one place a seer (*II.Chron.*xxix.30), and in the Greek version a prophet. He might thus be considered an antetype of the True Teacher.

A significant field of inquiry had most promisingly been opened up, which I tentatively explored as long ago as 1954. But I did not pursue the theme at the time. To be frank, I did not sufficiently appreciate its importance. Neither was I fully conscious of its ramifications. I had rather hoped that others, better equipped, would develop the subject. While this did not happen, aspects of it kept cropping up in specialist literature. It is only right to say that a great deal of research had been done over a long period into the provenance of Asaph documents in many languages, which had been known in the Near-East and in Europe from the Middle Ages. In these Asaph ben Berechiah is credited with a medical treatise, having links with the Hippocratic Oath. He is also regarded as an astronomer and astrologer. In this context Asaph is curiously linked with a John, son of Zebedee.

The Essenes, as is well-known, had considerable medical skill, and the treatise in question has recently been discovered to have points of contact with the Dead Sea Scrolls. For the Essenes the origins of medicine went back to Shem the son of Noah, and subsequently were handed down to members of the tribe of Levi, the priestly tribe.

But there was another line of inquiry, much more complex, which also had to be pursued. In one aspect this too related to a medieval work, one that had a very widespread circulation in Europe and Asia, the romance of *Barlaam and Joasaph*, where in the western version the account of the young prince Joasaph, converted to Christianity, proves largely to have been based on the life of the Buddha. Joasaph as Josaphat became a saint in the Christian calendar, and I was intrigued when I was at Mombasa in Kenya to encounter a native woodcarver of this name. The book was favoured in Europe by the heretical Cathars, who themselves had links with Essene teaching.

In the East ancient records told of the saintly teacher Jo-asaph or Yuz-Asaf, by some identified with Jesus, notably by the founder of the Ahmadiyya Movement. It was held that Jesus had survived the cross and travelled to the East to bring the Messianic Message to the Lost Ten Tribes of Israel, themselves identified with the Afghans and certain of the Kashmiris. The tomb of this Asaph personality is shown at Srinagar in Kashmir and it has been claimed as the ultimate tomb of Jesus.

A great deal has been written on this theme, and many venerable oriental texts cited, which I have employed with deep gratitude to the scholars of the Ahmadiyya Movement. The view that Jesus did not die on the cross was anciently asserted by Gnostic writers, and has recently been brought to the fore again in modern research, including that into the famous Turin Shroud, claimed to have covered the body of Jesus while in the tomb.

But the Asaph aspect was only one element demanding investigation. There was also the associated Joseph aspect. Using the account in the Bible of the favourite son of Jacob – whose death had been sought by his brothers and who had been exiled from his land – as a Messianic antetype, the Essenes saw in him the anticipation of their True Teacher. From this equation, and the doctrine of the two Messiahs, there emerged the figure of a 'Son of Joseph' Messiah as well as one who was 'Son of David', and who would precede him. He would be the Man performing the perfect will of God and suffering accordingly.

Higher flights of esotericism then linked the Man human with the

Man celestial, the primeval Son of Man, in whose universe-filling likeness the first man on earth, Adam, was created. A mythology of the last Times developed in which the era of World Peace and Justice would be signalled by Sky Man's final appearance on earth. It is a very widespread mythology credited in East and West, which has been given a new expression in our time by those who urge that superior beings from outer space will intervene to save the human race from self-destruction.

To say that I have been startled by the ramifications of the theme explored in this work would be a serious understatement. The problem has been how to arrange and present the material in a manner which would both assist elucidation and not be too difficult for the general reader to follow. I have sought to do my best, especially as very many people will be dealing with an intriguing mystery of which they have not previously been aware. I hope to guide them along the many strange and scattered trails, some of them overgrown and almost invisible. The legends and folklore of many climes and ages play their part in the story; but I have not developed, as too secondary, certain elements in Europe reflecting various arcane interests. I have touched on these where significant; but it was essential not to become side-tracked, however enticingly.

I have, of course, been conscious that much curious information reached the West through Islamic channels and through those who returned from the Crusades, as well as through the Jewish communities. A great deal was garbled and misinterpreted, because those whom it reached had an alien background in matters spiritual, and lacked the capacity to form a right judgement of what they received. They were also extremely credulous and gullible. I have alluded in the story to the Cathars, the Templars, the Freemasons and Rosicrucians, and to the legends of the Wandering Jew and Prester John. I do not doubt that in manuscripts which reached Europe, copies of which are in particular libraries, as well as in some still inaccessible monastic collections, there are additional sources to be tapped. Lost documents which we know about from allusions and quotations may yet come to light. Not a few have been given back to us in whole or part during the past century, and this in spite of the efforts of the ignorant and the hostile to suppress their contents.

Recently the authors of a book entitled *The Holy Blood and the Holy Grail*[2] have made reference to an alchemical work which had been in the possession of Nicolas Flamel, a Grand Master of the Priory of

Zion in the fourteenth century. Its title was: "The Sacred Book of Abraham the Jew, Prince, Priest, Levite, Astrologer and Philosopher, to that Tribe of Jews, who by the Wrath of God were dispersed among the Gauls." Whoever composed this book must have been familiar with certain Essene ideas and material. We have only to substitute the name Asaph for the conventional Jewish name Abraham to be back in the environment of Messianic ideas relating to the True Teacher. The researches in *The Holy Blood and the Holy Grail* have enabled me to amplify my European information, especially relating to the Templars and I most gladly acknowledge to the authors my gratitude for their explorations. Accordingly I have added an essential Appendix, *The Essenes and the Templars*.

Because the researches in which I have been for so long engaged affect Christian beliefs, and are also of general interest, I have endeavoured to make the presentation as uncomplicated as possible. Therefore, I have heavily reduced the weight of academic apparatus, and have furnished only the translations of texts from various languages. This will inflict no hardship on erudite colleagues, since the sources employed are everywhere stated and are accessible to them.

I gratefully express my indebtedness to many authorities. Where published material was concerned I have in every case specified the authors and publishers. Without these aids of many minds my undertaking would have been accomplished only with the very greatest difficulty. I should add that the essence of the book was the theme of the Claude Goldsmid Montefiore Lecture of 1982, which I was invited to deliver in London on June 9.

The ramifications of the theme are so extensive that what I have set down is far from exhaustive. But I hope the reader will share the excitement of the quest as we advance step by step along a very difficult road, pausing occasionally to look back on the way we have travelled. What has given the writer special pleasure is the realization of the extent to which different faiths and convictions have things in common. Manifestly it is practicable to achieve a large measure of unity in diversity. And this bodes well for the future of mankind. After all, as the Essenes help us to appreciate, we do have in Sky Man a common source of our being, who also is the guarantor of the fulfilment of our destiny.

*London* 1984                                    HUGH J. SCHONFIELD

# PART ONE

*Chapter One*

# The True Teacher

The quest in which we are to be engaged belongs to the realm of religious research and folklore. It takes its rise from a set of circumstances in the second century B.C., and particularly concerns a mysterious Jewish sect whom we have come to know as the Essenes. Much has been written about them, utilising ancient sources of reference. But we could not know them very effectively, because we were not on the inside. Only in modern times, as a result of the chance discovery of the Dead Sea Scrolls, have we been in a position to delve more deeply and clear up many former obscurities.

It is evident, however, that even now we are far from precise knowledge of what the Essenes represented and the extent of their influence. We might describe their position as related to the religious underground, connected with arcane mysteries and prophetic anticipations. These can to an extent be traced now from land to land and from century to century as this work will reveal. We shall often find ourselves in strange company, but as we pursue the quest the pieces will be found to assume a very significant shape.

At the beginning we must be occupied with origins, and it is here that we encounter that surprising figure, the True Teacher, whose unrecognised influence has extended down to the present day.

It is our experience that behind all the religions and philosophies with which we are familiar there has been an individual of substance, about whose life and activities – even if partly legendary – a certain amount can be known. We may think of Moses, of Confucius, of Zarathustra, of Gautama the Buddha, of Jesus and Mohammed. But one of the most intriguing revelations of the Dead Sea Scrolls was of the existence of a notable religious leader, revered by the Essenes, whose personal name was unrecorded, and who as yet has eluded positive identification with any individual in history. He was evidently a man of great spiritual and moral stature, worthy it would seem to rank with others highly venerated by mankind.

How could such a man have evaded the biographer's net? The

reasons are not far to seek. The collectivity of his followers constituted a restricted society, which dealt in mysteries, and deliberately
placed barriers in the path of the uninitiated by means of obscuring
devices and uncertain references. Consequently with the aid afforded
by the deciphering of the recovered manuscripts we have to endeavour somehow to puzzle out when he lived, and who conceivably he
may have been. But despite all that is now practicable the actual
identity of the one who is described in the records as the Unique, or
Singular, Teacher, or the True Teacher, still escapes us. However,
we do learn quite a few things about him.

On the positive side we can state with assurance from the evidences
that the Teacher was a Jew, of the priestly tribe of Levi, that he
functioned as both lawgiver and prophet, and was involved in combat-
ing religious laxity and apostasy. There is strong probability that he
was no mean poet, the composer of many hymns, often about his
own experiences. Certainly he was a man of great faith and piety.
For his activities he suffered persecution at the hands of the venal and
compromising high priests of his time, so that he was obliged to
forsake his country, and there were attempts made on his life.

From the available data we can deduce with reasonable assurance
that the Teacher was a contemporary of Judas Maccabaeus, leader of
the revolt against the anti-Judaic policies of the Seleucid ruler of
Palestine, Antiochus Epiphanes (175-164 B.C.). Judas was himself of
priestly family. A complication arises, however, in that there subsequently developed the expectation of a True Teacher of the Last
Days (the period immediately prior to the anticipated Messianic
Age), whose experiences would in many respects be comparable to
those of the previous Teacher, and who might even be his reincarnation. Some early Christians sought to relate the Teacher to Jesus.
These aspects have been very confusing to exegetes.

There has to be taken into account that many centuries before the
modern discovery of the Dead Sea Scrolls a number of books of the
Essenes and related sects, including the Christians, had obtained
widespread currency and had been translated into various languages.
In a number of cases the documents had been altered and interpolated
by those anxious to enlist the testimony of these holy books in the
cause of their own spiritual hero.

As a consequence, the deliberate design of the Essenes to guard the
True Teacher's incognito, on grounds both of veneration and policy,
was assisted by the desires of the interpolators. It was not only that

the date at which the True Teacher had lived, and what had befallen him, were obscured: but it was also by no means clear to scholars that allusion was being made in the recovered texts to a previously unknown individual.

Certain students of the Scrolls occupied themselves with seeking to identify the Teacher with someone already known to history, claiming particular persons as fitting in with the circumstances conveyed by the documents. The results were very diverse, and consequently inconclusive. The fact is that no one has given a generally accepted answer to the question, "Who was the True Teacher?" But at least it has come to be apprehended that there was such an individual, something which had not clearly registered before the discovery of the Scrolls.

With the Hebrew texts of the Scrolls in our possession, with their references to the Teacher and to his experiences, it could now be seen that certain familiar sources from ancient times had, it would seem, alluded to him, whereas previously they had not been understood in this light.

A typical example is the description of the Essenes furnished by the Jewish historian Josephus in the first century of the Christian era. He had attached himself to them for a time with the intention of being received as a member which he subsequently abandoned. The fact that he was of priestly stock would have commended him. In his account of the Essenes he mentions that: "After God they hold most in awe the name of their Lawgiver, any blasphemer of whom is punished with death."[1] Formerly it had been assumed that by the Lawgiver the Biblical Moses had been intended. Now that was by no means certain. Josephus had said "*their* Lawgiver" (the Lawgiver of the Essenes). We have no evidence that the name of Moses was held in special awe; but we do know that the name of the True Teacher was, so that his actual name is still a mystery. He had been a Levite, regarded as the promised prophet like Moses (*Deut*.xviii.18-19), the architect of the New Covenant.

There was another reference to be found in an Essenite work, *The Testaments of the XII Patriarchs* (i.e. the sons of Jacob). This was pre-Christian, but in available manuscripts it is considerably interpolated by Christian hands. The passage occurs appropriately in the *Testament of Levi*, and reads as follows:

And now I have learnt that for seventy weeks (*Dan*.ix.24) ye shall go astray and profane the priesthood and pollute the sacrifices. And ye shall make void the Law, and set at naught the words of the Prophets by evil perverseness. And ye shall persecute righteous men, and hate the godly; the words of the faithful shall ye abhor. And a man who reneweth the Law in the power of the Most High ye shall call a deceiver; and at last ye shall rush upon him to slay him, not knowing his dignity, taking innocent blood through wickedness upon your heads. And your holy places shall be laid waste even to the ground because of him. And ye shall have no place that is clean; but ye shall be among the Gentiles a curse and a dispersion until He shall again visit you, and in pity receive you.[2]

Dr R.H. Charles, whose translation I have employed, regarded the sentence commencing, "And a man who reneweth the Law . .", as conceivably a Christian interpolation. And he noted, "We have no means of discovering this reference." But Charles was writing forty years before the find of the Dead Sea Scrolls, in view of which the Renewer of the Law can be identified with the Lawgiver of the Essenes, the True Teacher, whose experiences are here mentioned. The latter part of the quotation could indeed have been overworked, like other parts of the *Testaments*, by Christians who sought to identify the True Teacher with Jesus.

In setting down as much as they could about the True Teacher while safeguarding his name, the Essene scribes had done their work well. We can learn an appreciable amount about his activities, and discover when he was operative; but he has to remain at least relatively nameless. This is the conclusion I have reached after many years of research. But it has also become clear that his advent and activities gave rise, under Essene influence, to the formulation of the terms of a developed Messianic personality. The outcome of this was that it became possible to see in several notable individuals who arose subsequently the need to accentuate their conformity with the True Teacher's character and experiences. They were seen as either the mysterious True Teacher himself, or as his End Time successor.

The process of transference worked the other way also. The Teacher's story drew to itself elements of the experiences of much earlier saintly personalities related in the Bible. The consequence was that, deriving from the saga of the True Teacher, Messianic speculation and expectation was increased by an extra ingredient, sponsored by, and mostly peculiar to, the eclectic groups having some kinship with the Essenes and influenced by certain of their books.

A new mythology began to take shape around the character of a Levitical hero, Prophet, Priest and Legislator,[3] having Messianic attributes and significance, and whose sufferings were expiatory for those who believed in him. There emerged a composite, partly legendary figure, whose impress on human convictions was to become so widespread and prolonged that it still has currency today.

In Part 2 we shall be pursuing our investigations in numerous directions and epochs. But first of all we must delve into the circumstances which brought forth the Teacher, and deduce what we can of his character and contribution from the sources now available.

### Chapter Two

# The Time of Wrath

There is no serious problem in ascertaining the circumstances among the Jews which led up to and embraced the activities of the True Teacher. We have historical records in the books of *Maccabees* in the Apocrypha, and in the *Antiquities of the Jews* of Flavius Josephus. We also have fairly straightforward accounts in Essenite documents which reflect the same period, and there are certain supplementary sources of information.

Since the conquests of Alexander the Great the Jews had come into much closer contact with the Hellenic world, and their intellectuals were not unresponsive to its influences. Inevitably they were involved in the rivalry and power struggle of Alexander's successors, the Ptolemies of Egypt and the Seleucids of Syria. By the beginning of the second century B.C. the Seleucids won the day so far as Palestine was concerned, and it became an adjunct of the Seleucid Empire. The Jewish high priests and their Council continued to act as the responsible government of the country; but, as with the Roman Papacy in the Middle Ages, ambition and avarice ate into the spirtual fabric of the State.

As a consequence a purifying reform movement was bound to manifest itself in priestly circles, inspired by individuals who were horrified by the insidious inroads of paganism and venality. The movement became known as that of the Chasidim (the Pious), a body of Jewish Puritans, which came into being early in the second century B.C. in what was described as the 'Time of Wrath'.

In the Testamentary Document incorporated in the *Damascus Document* of the Essenes we read how, in spite of apostasies, God "left a remnant to Israel, and did not give them over to destruction. But in the Time of Wrath He visited them (390 years after He had given them into the hands of Nebuchadnezzar, the King of Babylon)." The text then continues:

> And He caused to spring forth from Israel and Aaron
> A root of His planting to inherit the land,

And they had understanding of their iniquity,
And they knew they were guilty men.
And they were like the blind,
And them that grope their way, for twenty years.
And God considered their works;
For they sought Him with a perfect heart.
And He raised up for them a Teacher of Righteousness[1]
To lead them in the way of His heart.
And He made known to succeeding generations
What He would do to the last generation,
To a perfidious congregation:
Those who turn aside out of the way.
This is the time of which it was written,
'As a stubborn heifer, Israel behaved himself stubbornly,'[2]
When there arose a Scoffer,
Who distilled for Israel deceptive waters,
And caused them to stray in the trackless wilderness,
To suppress the old paths,
So as to turn aside from the right ways.
And remove the landmarks the fathers had set in their inheritance:
So as to make cleave to them the curses of His covenant;[3]
So that He should deliver them to the sword
That avengeth His covenant;
Because they sought after flatteries and chose deceit,
And kept watch for breaches.
They laid waste the best of the flock,
And justified the wicked and condemned the righteous;
And transgressed the covenant and violated the statute,
And attacked the soul of the righteous.
And all that walked uprightly their soul abhorred,
And they pursued them with the sword,
And rejoiced in the strife of the people.
And so the wrath of God was kindled against their congregation,
So that He laid waste all their multitude,
And their deeds were uncleanness before Him.[4]

It is quite clear here that the Teacher of Righteousness, the True Teacher, rose at a time which pious Jews denounced as one of spiritual wickedness and apostasy. So great was the evil that it merited the wrath of God and the operation of the curses set down in *Deuteronomy*. The only period of Jewish history with which it could be compared was that of the waywardness and idolatry in the 6th century B.C., which brought about the destruction of the Temple and the Babylonian Exile in the time of Nebuchadnezzar.

The author of *I.Maccabees* furnishes us with the historical background, and establishes that the Time of Wrath with which the

*Damascus Document* is concerned is definitely to be dated in the reign of the Seleucid ruler Antiochus IV, Epiphanes, whom the author terms 'a sinful root'. He came to the throne in 175 B.C.

In those days, he writes, lawless men came forth from Israel, and misled many, saying, 'Let us go and make a covenant with the Gentiles round about us, for since we separated from them many evils have come upon us.' This proposal pleased them, and some of the people eagerly went to the king. He authorized them to observe the ordinances of the Gentiles. So they built a gymnasium in Jerusalem, according to Gentile custom, and removed the marks of circumcision, and abandoned the holy covenant. They joined with the Gentiles and sold themselves to do evil ... But many in Israel stood firm and were resolved in their hearts not to eat unclean food. They chose to die rather than to be defiled by food or to profane the holy covenant, and they did die. And very great wrath came upon Israel.[5]

There is a passage to the same effect in the pre-Christian Essenite document the *Assumption of Moses*.

And when the times of chastisement draw nigh and vengeance arises through the kings that share in their guilt and punish them (i.e. the Jews), they themselves also will be divided as to the truth. Wherefore it hath come to pass; 'They will turn aside from righteousness, and approach iniquity, and they will defile with pollutions the house of their worship,' and 'they will go a whoring after strange gods.' For they will not follow the truth of God, but some will pollute the altar with the very gifts which they offer to the Lord, (they) who are not priests but slaves, sons of slaves. And many in those times will respect the persons of the rich, and be greedy of gain ... and the borders of their habitation will be filled with lawless deeds and iniquities: they will forsake the Lord ...
And there will come upon them a second visitation[6] and wrath, such as had not befallen them from the beginning until that time, in which he will stir up against them the king of the kings of the earth and one who ruleth with great power (i e. Antiochus Epiphanes), who will crucify those who confess to their circumcision: and those who conceal it he will torture and deliver them to be bound and led into prison ... and they will be forced by goads to blaspheme with insolence the Name, and finally after these things the laws and what they had above their altar.[7]

Each of the sources – and there are others – identifies the Time of Wrath with the same set of circumstances; so that we are on firm ground. The period is well-defined and we are aware of much that happened in it.

There is further agreement. As we have seen from the quotations from *I.Maccabees*, what brought about 'the Wrath' was the initiative taken by eminent and well-to-do Jews in advising Antiochus that they wished to follow the way of life of the other peoples under his rule. The persecution of the Jews, with the commission of terrible atrocities, was the outcome of the king's favourable response to these overtures, when the faithful in Israel refused to act against their religion. It is with reference to the Hellenizers that the *Damascus Document* introduces 'the Scoffer' of our quotation, who led Israel astray, and who is elsewhere described as 'the Wicked Priest'.

In the *Habakkuk Commentary* among the Dead Sea Scrolls, at *Hab*.ii.5-6, the Essene interpretation is:

This refers to the Wicked Priest, who was called by the Name of Truth at the commencement of his office. But when he ruled Israel his heart was lifted up and he forsook God; and he betrayed the statutes because of riches, and he despoiled and amassed the riches of violent men who rebelled against God. And he took the riches of peoples to increase his iniquitous guilt, and followed abominable ways in every kind of foul impurity.

From the same work we may quote *Hab*.ii.17:

For the violence inflicted on Lebanon shall return upon thee, and the oppression exercised against the cattle shall fan (the flame), because of the human blood which has been shed and the violence which has been inflicted on the country, on the city, and on all that dwell therein.

The explanation is:

This refers to the Wicked Priest, to reward him for the recompense he has repaid to the Poor; for 'Lebanon' is the Party of the Community, and 'the cattle' are the simple in Judah who practise the Law. And God shall condemn him to destruction, even as he purposed to destroy the Poor. And when it is said, 'because of the blood shed in the city and the violence inflicted on the country,' 'the city' refers to Jerusalem in which the Wicked Priest has done abominable deeds and has profaned the Sanctuary. As to 'violence inflicted on the country', this means the towns of Judah in which he robbed the Poor of their substance.

Our sources clearly indicate that the Wicked Priest who provoked the wrath of God represents the contemporary high priesthood, which was in a position of authority in the nation, and as God's minister he was expected to set an example of righteousness and faithfulness to the Law. In fact at this period three successive high priests are presented to us as shocking characters, leaders in the corruption of their people. Their adopted Hellenic names were Jason, Menelaus and Alcimus. In the character of the Wicked Priest of the Scrolls it is likely that we have a composite representation of all three, but more particularly Alcimus.

Before commenting further it is important to note that the manner in which the Gospels interpret the Old Testament is of the same order as that employed by the Essenes. Similarly the early Christians were also concerned with the opposing forces of Good and Evil.[8] The idea of the Cosmic Drama had been an inheritance from the Zoroastrian faith when the Jews were under Persian rule.

Following the Essenes the Christians also employed the term 'the Poor' to represent the faithful in opposition to the wealthy 'Sinners'. And of course individuals who joined such communities did hand over their possessions.[9] One Essene type of Judaeo-Christian sect became known as the Ebionites, the term being derived from the Hebrew word for 'the poor'. There was a close relationship between the Essenes and early Christians as will be made increasingly clear; and they shared antagonism to the rich, powerful and venal chief priests. The Christian hero had been brought to his death by them as the True Teacher had been.

In our investigation we have always to bear in mind that the figures brought before us in Essenite literature are both particular individuals or groups, and also types of Good or Evil. For this reason we must not press personal identifications too closely, and we can see why it is so difficult positively to distinguish particular historical characters. There were even attempts to accommodate the likeness of one personality to that of an earlier one, or to descriptions of him, on the assumption that the earlier references had been prophetic anticipations. The True Teacher himself may partly in this respect be the fulfilment of an antetype, and representative of certain attributes.

With this literature we are in the realm of the morality play, but not of pure fiction. We are dealing with the personification of opposing forces of Good and Evil, Light and Darkness, a tradition still reflected in our Christmas pantomimes and in oriental morality plays.

### Chapter Three

# The Evildoers

The story of the Great Apostasy which brought down the wrath of God belongs to the second quarter of the second century B.C. in the reigns of Antiochus Epiphanes, his son Antiochus Eupator, and after him Demetrius Soter. We have already reported on some of the circumstances – the activities of the Jewish Hellenizers – which were conducive to the design to suppress the practice of Judaism. Now we must more particularly represent the conduct of the high priests of that time, Jason, Menelaus and Alcimus, as they are depicted in the records. It is essential to do this because in the Scrolls it is the Wicked Priest who persecutes the True Teacher and his following.

Our primary historical sources are *I* and *II Maccabees* in the Biblical Apocrypha, and Book XII of Josephus's *Antiquities of the Jews*. *II Maccabees* is not, as might be supposed, the continuation of *I Maccabees*, but an entirely different work, an abridgment of part of a much larger work by Jason of Cyrene, now lost. Josephus largely depends on *I Maccabees*, though in places he deviates from this authority. The viewpoint of *II Maccabees* comes closest to that of the Dead Sea Scrolls. It is more exotic in its reporting of dreams and visions, and acts of Divine intervention, and is very decidedly on the side of the angels in its attitude towards the evildoers.

As we have noted, the Jewish high priests with whom we are concerned all adopted Greek names in their desire to conform to the Greek way of life. Jesus became Jason, and Onias became Menelaus. Less familiarly Alcimus probably bore the Hebrew name of Joachim. All three were ambitious for power and prestige, and as the spiritual leaders of their nation they set the worst possible example. We have to report on this in detail.

The first offender was Jason. He had obtained the high priesthood from King Antiochus by bribery, and then sought to convert Israel to Hellenism.

With alacrity he founded a gymnasium right under the citadel, and he induced the noblest of the young men to wear the Greek hat. There was such an extreme of Hellenization and increase in the adoption of foreign ways because of the surpassing wickedness of Jason, who was ungodly and no high priest, that the priests were no longer intent upon their service at the altar. Despising the Sanctuary and neglecting the sacrifices, they hastened to take part in the unlawful proceedings in the wrestling arena after the call to the discus, disdaining the honours prized by their fathers, and putting the highest value upon Greek forms of prestige.

But having supplanted his own brother, Onias III, Jason was in turn supplanted by Menelaus, who was not of the lineage of the high priests. Menelaus, being sent as an emissary of Jason with funds for Antiochus, took the opportunity to outbid Jason and obtain the high priesthood for himself. Jason was driven into exile.

Menelaus, however, having taken office, was not so keen to keep his bargain. But he did not scruple to rob the Temple at Jerusalem of its treasures to secure his own position. While Antiochus was dealing with a revolt in the north, Menelaus – according to the author of *II Maccabees* – bribed Andronicus, the king's deputy, with gold vessels from the Temple to murder the legitimate high priest, Onias III, who was Jason's brother, and who had taken refuge at Daphne near Antioch. Onias had not hesitated to denounce the sacrilegious acts of Menelaus. The crime was so shocking that Antiochus ordered the execution of Andronicus. But Menelaus was not touched. "He remained in office," says our authority, "because of the cupidity of those in power, growing in wickedness, having become the chief plotter against his fellow citizens."

Shortly after this Antiochus invaded Egypt for the second time. Rumours of his death reached Jerusalem, and induced the deposed Jason to make an assault on the city, both in his interest and perhaps to avenge the murder of his brother.

The attack, in which thousands of Jews died, proved abortive however. Jason became a hunted man, fleeing from place to place, and finally he was cast ashore in Egypt. "He who had driven many from their country into exile died in exile . . . He who had cast out many to lie unburied had no one to mourn for him; he had no funeral of any sort and no place in the tomb of his fathers."

Antiochus returned from Egypt believing Judaea was in revolt. His troops stormed Jerusalem and slaughtered men, women and children. Eighty thousand are said to have perished, and as many again were taken captive and sold into slavery. The king dared to enter the holy Temple guided by Menelaus, "who had become a traitor both to the laws and to his country,' and, seizing its sacred treasures, Antiochus returned to Antioch.

It was shortly after this that the king decreed that the Jewish Temple should be converted to the worship of Zeus Olympius. The holy place was given over to "abominations that make desolate" (*Dan*.ix.27). Now began, reputedly with the connivance of Menelaus, the great desecration and persecution associated with the name of Antiochus Epiphanes. The author of *II Maccabees* records:

Harsh and utterly grievous was the onslaught of evil. For the Temple was filled with debauchery and revelling of the Gentiles, who dallied with harlots and had intercourse with women within the sacred precincts, and besides brought in things for sacrifices that were unfit. The altar was covered with abominable offerings which were forbidden by the laws. A man could neither keep the sabbath, nor observe the feasts of his fathers, nor so much as confess himself a Jew (vi.3-6).

In the great attack on their religion the Jews found a champion in Judas Maccabaeus, who led a revolt, and by his daring exploits finally secured for his people their freedom of worship by decree of Antiochus Eupator, son and successor of Epiphanes. The tyrant's miserable end is circumstantially recorded, as is that of the apostate Menelaus not long afterwards. The latter had succeeded by his duplicity in retaining a measure of authority for some years; but his misdeeds finally caught up with him. It was said that his policies had forced the Jews into revolt. He was sent to Beroea (Aleppo) to be executed by being hurled from a high tower onto a bed of ashes. "And this," says the record, "was eminently just; because he had committed many sins against the altar whose fire and ashes were holy, he met his death in ashes."

The acts of Antiocus V (Eupator) were really those of his guardian, Lysias, since the king was only a child. Both were done away with by the next Seleucid monarch Demetrius I (Soter) in 162 B.C. It was in his reign that there flourished the third of the 'Wicked Priests', Alcimus. He was by no means the most culpable of the trio; but he appears more prominently in the records as the enemy of the Saints, the so-called Chasidim, who by this time were an organized body, and he approximates more nearly to the 'Wicked Priest' who perse-cuted the 'True Teacher'.[2] He is introduced by the author of *II Maccabees* as a "certain Alcimus, who had formerly been high priest, but had wilfully defiled himself in the times of separation. This is very like what is said of the Wicked Priest in the Essene

*Commentary on Habakkuk* (ii. 5-6): "This concerns the Wicked Priest, who was called by the Name of Truth when he first arose. But when he ruled Israel his heart became proud, and he forsook God and betrayed the precepts for the sake of riches."

With the take over of the country by the armed forces of Demetrius an invitation was sent to Alcimus to advise on the attitude of the Jews towards the Syrian regime. Alcimus at once saw his opportunity to gain, or regain, the high priesthood, and he is credited with this response:

Those of the Jews who are called Hasidaeans (Chasidim), whose leader is Judas Maccabaeus, are keeping up war and stirring up sedition, and will not let the kingdom attain tranquillity. Therefore I have laid aside my ancestral glory – I mean the high priesthood – and have now come here, first because I am genuinely concerned for the interests of the king, and second because I have regard also for my fellow citizens. For through the folly of those whom I have mentioned our whole nation is now in no small misfortune. Since you are acquainted, O king, with the details of the matter, deign to take thought for our country and our hard-pressed nation with the gracious kindness which you show to all. For as long as Judas lives, it is impossible for the government to find peace.[3]

Thereupon Demetrius appointed Nicanor, one of his commanders, governor of Judaea, and sent him to Jerusalem with an army to kill Judas and install Alcimus as high priest. When Nicanor came to Jerusalem, he temporised, having respect for Judas and his valour, and came to terms with him.

This did not suit Alcimus at all, whose aim was to destroy Judas, and he reported Nicanor to the king. Nicanor was ordered to seize Judas without delay and send him as a prisoner to Antioch. In the event Judas had his suspicions of Nicanor's intentions, and escaped from Jerusalem. Later with relatively small forces, Judas defeated the army of Nicanor, who died in battle. The day was annually celebrated by the Jews. This is the account given by the author of *II Maccabees*.

A more detailed and somewhat different account is given in *I Maccabees*. Here Alcimus played a more prominent part. King Demetrius sent Bacchides, one of his friends and governor of the province Beyond-the-River (i.e. the Euphrates), to Jerusalem with an army. His mission was to install Alcimus, who accompanied him, as high priest and governor of Judaea.

At Jerusalem a group of scribes, stated to be Hasidaeans, came out as an embassy to ask for terms, for they said, "A priest of the line of Aaron has come with the army, and he will not harm us." But treacherously sixty of them were seized and slaughtered. The narrator sees in this event the fulfilment of *Psalm* lxxix.2-3, "The flesh of thy saints and their blood they poured out round about Jerusalem, and there was none to bury them."[4]

Bacchides now departed, leaving Alcimus in charge of Judaea. But Judas and his men effectively conducted a resistance movement; so that Alcimus was forced to seek further assistance from King Demetrius. It was then that the king sent Nicanor with another army to support Alcimus and destroy Judas; and when the battle was finally joined the greatly superior forces of Nicanor were defeated and he himself was slain.

Learning of this disaster Demetrius put another major force into the field under Bacchides and Alcimus. Faced with the might of this army many of Judas's men deserted; but he refused to abandon the unequal contest. The battle raged from morning to evening, but before it ended Judas was killed. The year was B.C. 160.

The death of the hero enabled Bacchides and Alcimus to take vengeance on the demoralised Jewish loyalists. "And thus," says the author of *I Maccabees*, "there was great distress in Israel, such as had not been since the time that prophets ceased to appear among them" (IX.27).

But the triumph of the most notable of the Wicked Priests was short-lived. At Jerusalem in the following year (B.C. 159) Alcimus gave orders to tear down the wall of the inner court of the Temple. The text continues:

> But he only began to tear it down, for at that time Alcimus was stricken and his work was hindered; his mouth was stopped and he was paralysed, so that he could no longer say a word or give commands concerning his house. And Alcimus died at that time in great agony.[5] When Bacchides saw that Alcimus was dead, he returned to the king, and the land had rest for two years" (*I Macc*.IX.54-57).

We now have before us the historical period and the principal circumstances which called forth the manifestation of the True Teacher, particularly as they relate to the iniquity and apostasy of the spiritual leaders of Israel, God's anointed high priests. Such turpitude with its consequent dire tribulations could only mean that the climax of the Ages was approaching. The Enemy of Souls was now putting forward his utmost efforts to defeat and destroy the forces of Good which were faithful to God and His laws.

It is not too difficult to imagine the reactions, the passionate and prophetic zeal, which animated the faithful and produced pious leaders like Judas Maccabaeus, himself of priestly stock. We turn, then, to look at significant personalities in the camp of the righteous resisters. They should enable us to get on the track of the True Teacher, even if they do not directly disclose him. He must have removed to the Land of Damascus around B.C. 160 in Israel's time of supreme distress following the death of Judas Maccabaeus.

*Chapter Four*

# The Resisters

In the books of *Maccabees* various individuals are brought before us as representative of the Resistance. They are persons who adhered firmly to their ancestral faith in the period of persecution and apostasy, refusing all inducements to forsake Judaism. Many of them boldly denounced the evildoers, often taking up arms against them, or, as individuals, they suffered torture and death as martyrs.

Among those who are singled out for record we shall now look at particular persons who may at least partially reflect the one referred to by the Essenes as the True Teacher. We might think to include the heroic Judas Maccabaeus, since in various respects he would seem to qualify. He is described in *II Maccabees* as leader of the Hasidaeans, the Pious in Israel. He was a redoubtable opponent of one of the Wicked Priests. He received many tokens of Divine favour, and cleansed the defiled Temple at Jerusalem. Finally he died in battle against the forces supporting the high priest Alcimus. But the True Teacher is not represented to us in the Dead Sea Scrolls as a military commander.

We shall have more to say of Judas, and of course we must mention here his father, the priest Mattathias. When the Temple at Jerusalem was desecrated and given over to the worship of Zeus by order of Antiochus Epiphanes he is said to have cried, "Alas! Why was I born to see this, the ruin of my people, the ruin of the holy city, and to dwell there when it was given over to the enemy?" He and his sons rent their clothes as a sign of mourning and put on sackcloth, and retired to their ancestral home at Modein.

But to Modein came the king's officers to enforce the offering of heathen sacrifices on an altar which was erected. Mattathias and his family were called upon to participate; but they refused to depart from their religion. When a Jew in the crowd came forward to submit, Mattathias ran and slew him upon the altar, and then after him the king's officer, and he tore down the altar.

Then we read that "Mattathias cried out in the city with a loud voice, saying, 'Let every man who is zealous for the Law and supports the Covenant come out with me!' And he and his sons fled to the hills and left all that they had in the city" (*I Macc.*ii).

In those days many faithful Jews with their families took to the wilderness, here they were hunted down and killed – often on the Sabbath when they would not defend themselves. Mattathias and his supporters, organizing resistance, decided therefore to authorise fighting on the Sabbath in self-defence. To this apparently some of the most pious, the Chasidim, agreed. Mattathias does not seem to have suffered martyrdom. He is said to have died a natural death in B.C. 160 and was buried in his native town of Modein. Of his five sons he nominated the third, Judas, to take command of the resistance because of his military prowess.

One who was martyred at this time was a certain Eleazar, spoken of as one of the scribes occupying a high position (*II Macc.*vi). He refused to eat swine's flesh, and was tortured by the agents of Antiochus. He was in his ninetieth year, and died on the rack. He is quoted as saying, "By manfully giving up my life now, I will show myself worthy of my old age, and leave to the young a noble example of how to die a good death willingly and nobly for the revered and holy laws."

The account of Eleazar is followed immediately by another relating to the martyrdom of a mother and her seven sons, who all refused to eat swine's flesh. The testimony of each one is recorded.

We have here examples – and there are others – of those at this period who signally gave their lives for their religion. They may be said to have a certain affinity with the True Teacher, and to an extent bring us closer to him.

This perhaps was in the mind of the later Essenite author of the *Assumption of Moses*, to which we have already referred, who was writing near the beginning of the first century A.D. In the prediction of the persecution by Antiochus Epiphanes he makes Moses foretell:

Then in that day there will be a man of the tribe of Levi, whose name will be TAXO, who having seven sons will speak to them exhorting them: 'Observe, my sons, behold a second ruthless and unclean visitation has come upon the people, and a punishment merciless and far exceeding the first.[1] For what nation or region or what people of those who are impious towards the Lord, who have done many abominations, have suffered as great calamities as have befallen us? Now therefore, my sons, hear me: for observe and know that neither did our fathers nor their forefathers tempt God, so as to transgress His commands. And ye know that this is our strength, and thus will we do. Let us fast for the space of three days, and on the fourth let us go into a cave which is in the field, and let us die rather than transgress the commands of the Lord of lords, the God of our fathers. For if we do this and die, our blood will be avenged before the Lord.'[2]

Here the effects of the persecution are singularly exemplified in the testimony of a pious Jew of the priestly tribe of Levi. He is a symbolic rather than an actual person, and the name given him is deliberately cryptic, conveying or hinting at a particular individual.[3] In a way he is a composite of the Resisters. TAXO has seven sons. The priest Mattathias had five sons; but we have also noted the martyrdom of the woman with seven sons. We do not have to take the number literally: it is the sacred seven.

The manner of the death of TAXO and his sons is not stated. They could have starved or committed suicide. In Palestine, in times of war or stress people made use of the numerous caves as hideouts and places of refuge. What is of moment, apart from the mysterious name, is that the individual referred to was of Levitic descent, possibly a priest, as was the True Teacher of the Dead Sea Scrolls who manifested himself around this period. It was among the pious priests and Levites, the Chasidim, opposing the apostates, that the Teacher would have found his followers, and did find them according to the *Damascus Document*.[4]

The True Teacher of the Scrolls was persecuted by the Wicked Priest. This could be said to have happened in the case of Judas Maccabaeus. But, as we have noted, we have no evidence that the Teacher took up arms or was politically involved as a man of action. What is more, of all the Resisters of whom we are taking note none of them left Palestine as did the Teacher. Yet we may feel that in what is related of Judas Maccabaeus and others a certain community with the True Teacher was intended, as being individuals of the same order, and notably in respect of being a priestly Chasid. We have to accommodate ourselves to the ramifications of Essene crypticism.

As regards Judas Maccabaeus he is depicted as a man of piety and prayer and also as a visionary. We shall have more of this to adduce in Part One Chapters VII and X. But we observe here that he is singled out in the records we have cited as the object of hostility of the wicked high priest Alcimus, the one who most nearly represents the Wicked Priest of the Dead Sea Scrolls.

With the activities of Alcimus are associated the betrayal and murder of an embassy of sixty of the Chasidim. And here we have to turn to Rabbinical sources, from which we learn of another conceivable candidate for the rôle of the mysterious Teacher. This man too is stated to háve been "a Chasid belonging to the priesthood,"[6] and according to tradition was an uncle of Alcimus. The name of this individual was Joseph (Jose) son of Joezer of Zeredah. He was an eminent transmitter of Jewish teaching in direct succession from the saintly high priest Simon the Just. A saying of his is quoted in the *Mishnah*: "Let thy house be a meeting-place for the wise. Powder thyself in the dust of their feet, and drink in their words with avidity" (*Aboth*.i.4).

This Joseph (Jose) was a known opponent of Hellenism. He is said to have declared as unclean all countries outside the land of Israel, in order to dissuade Jews from emigrating (*Shab*.46a). It is highly probable that he was a member of the deputation to Alcimus and Bacchides of Chasidic priests who were executed.[7] At any rate, according to an early *Midrash* he suffered martyrdom, and on the way to execution this dialogue took place between him and Alcimus.

Said Alcimus, "See the profit and honours that have fallen to my lot in consequence of what I have done, whilst thou for thy obstinacy hast the misfortune to die as a criminal." Joseph replied, "If such is the lot of those who anger God, what shall be the lot of those who carry out His will?" Alcimus retorted, "Is there anyone who has carried out His will more than thou?" To this Joseph made answer, "If this (i.e. my martyrdom) is the end of those who carry out His will, what awaits those who anger Him?" Thereupon Alcimus was smitten with remorse and died.

Examining the records of those eminent Jews who suffered for their Faith in the 'Time of Wrath' we do not find one who answers fully to the personality and experiences of the True Teacher as represented in the Dead Sea Scrolls. The one who may be thought to come closest is the last we have looked at, and he in particular enables us to move a step forward in our quest for enlightenment.

But along the way we have travelled so far there have been several hidden pointers to the personality, if not to the identity, of the True Teacher. We shall now begin to disclose these as they are fundamental to the creation of the Teacher's Messianic significance.

*Chapter Five*

# The Joseph Connection

There is some biographical information about the True Teacher which is to be found in the Dead Sea Scrolls, and which would seem dependable. He was an outspoken champion of the Divine Laws, and as such was hated and detested by the Wicked Priest of his day, almost certainly Alcimus. We can be confident that he was a priest, and highly gifted as a prophet and poet. In the Essene *Commentary on Habakkuk* (on *Hab*.ii.1) we read that the Teacher was one "to whom God made known all the mysteries of the words of His servants the Prophets." He would seem to be identical with the Priest "in whom God set understanding, that he might interpret all the words of His servants the Prophets, through whom He foretold all that would happen to His people and His land" (on *Hab*.i.3).

We learn from the Scrolls that he led his followers out into the wilderness like a second Moses to enable them to observe the laws of God in purity, requiring them to enter into a New Covenant in the Land of Damascus, following the intimation of the Prophet Jeremiah (xxxi.31).[1] The time of this exodus can be dated with some assurance.[2] The Teacher and his followers were not left in peace in their place of refuge, and attempts were made by the Wicked Priest to compass their destruction. While the death of the True Teacher is nowhere described, it is perhaps suggested, and there are some indications that it could have been brought about by his adversaries.

While whatever we can discover about the life of the True Teacher is valuable – both when he lived and the circumstances of his career – we need to appreciate that, as with John the Baptist and Jesus, we are viewing him through the eyes of his followers as a figure larger than life. And he is even more elusive because of the deliberate design of the secretive Essenes who venerated him and would not even refer to him by his real name. A Messianic mythology became attached to him, as we shall later demonstrate, which captured the imagination of generations, who hoped for the End Time in which he would reincarnate or manifest himself to bring to pass the final victory of the Good.

In the interim, two representative personal names were communicated to the faithful as symbolic of the Teacher's qualities. Under one of these the Teacher appears as the Suffering Servant of God, while under the other he is the Inspired Seer. There is an inter-relationship between the names and the rôles, as we shall disclose. The first name is JOSEPH.

The personality and experiences of the Biblical Patriarch Joseph had a great appeal for the Chasidim, and subsequently for the Rabbis. He was seen as the *Zadik gamur*, the perfect righteous man, who is at the same time the innocent sufferer. According to the Rabbis he was well-versed in the *Torah*: he was a prophet, and the Holy Spirit dwelt in him from childhood to the day of his death.[3] In the Blessings of the XII Patriarchs in *Genesis* xlix, and of their tribes in *Deuteronomy* xxxiii, Joseph is singled out for special mention and encomiums. In both he is presented as "him that was separated from his brethren."

Joseph in the Bible is the innocent one, a man of dreams and visions, whom his brothers hated and wished to kill. Sold into slavery, he rose to eminence in a strange land, and ultimately became the instrument of his family's salvation. Abandoned, and declared to have perished, in due time he manifested himself – as it were from the dead – in the hour of his people's need.

Here for the Essenes was a significant antetype of the True Teacher. From their records it can be gleaned that the Wicked Priest sought to kill the Teacher; but initially at least he escaped this fate and survived in exile. The legend arose that he would reappear, manifesting himself as the True Teacher of the Last Times.

It becomes important to see how the Patriarch Joseph is presented by the Essenes in their literature. In the *Book of Jubilees* it is stated that the Jewish fast day, the solemn Day of Atonement in the autumn, was instituted with reference to him.

And the sons of Jacob slaughtered a kid, and dipped the coat of Joseph in the blood, and sent it to Jacob their father on the tenth of the seventh month . . . For this reason it is ordained for the Children of Israel that they should afflict themselves on the tenth of the seventh month – on the day that the news which made him weep for Joseph came to Jacob his father – that they should make atonement for themselves with a young goat on the tenth of the seventh month, once a year, for their sins (xxxiv. 12. 18).

We may well ask whether there is more in this than meets the eye? Why should the reported death of Joseph be linked with the Day of Atonement, since in fact Joseph had not died? We may note that a rather obscure passage in the Essene *Commentary on the Prophet Habakkuk* (ii.15) links the persecution of the True Teacher by the Wicked Priest with the Day of Atonement, and it could have significance that the high priest Alcimus as we have recorded,[4] was responsible for the death of the priest and Chasid Joseph, son of Joezer.

But we meet with an even more curious passage in the *Testaments of the XII Patriarchs*, a work in which allusions to the True Teacher have been detected.[5] The passage we wish to quote here is in the *Testament of Benjamin*, and purports to relate to the Patriarch Joseph. The texts of the manuscripts differ, and we give that which is most reliable. The speaker is Joseph's younger brother Benjamin.

Do ye also, therefore, my children, love the Lord God of heaven and earth, and keep His commandments, following the example of the holy and good man Joseph. For until his death he was not willing to tell regarding himself; but Jacob, having learnt it from the Lord, told it to him. Nevertheless he kept denying it. And then with difficulty he was persuaded by the adjurations of Israel (i.e. Jacob). For Joseph also besought our father that he would pray for his brethren, that the Lord would not impute to them as sin whatever evil they had done unto him.[6] And thus Jacob cried out: 'My good child, thou hast prevailed over the bowels of thy father Jacob.' And he embraced and kissed him for two hours, saying 'In thee shall be fulfilled the prophecy of Heaven, which says that the blameless one shall be defiled for lawless men, and the sinless one shall die for godless men.'

But the prophecy cited, evidently from some unknown written source, could not apply to the Biblical Joseph, any more than the Day of Atonement could reflect the representation of Joseph as having died, when he had actually been sold into slavery. Under the figure of Joseph we are surely meant to discern someone else, conceivably the True Teacher, who suffered at the hands of lawless and godless men, and whose believed death was supposed to bring atonement. That the prediction relates to a Joseph-type was discerned by a Christian interpolater of the *Testaments*: for after the words "prophecy of Heaven" he inserted the words, "concerning the Lamb of God and Saviour of the world", so relating the prediction to Jesus.

It is worthy of note that in another work, the heavily Christianised *Ascension of Isaiah*, a list of the Hebrew prophets is given whose books are in the Bible. After Malachi the author adds two more, Joseph the Just and Daniel.[8] Daniel we know, but who is Joseph the Just to whom a book of prophecy is ascribed?

Somehow the Joseph figure under Essene influence came to have

Messianic significance, and this could be because of the priestly status of the True Teacher. In Israel both the high priests and the kings were anointed ones (messiahs equals christs), the "sons of oil" of *Zechariah* iv. Their offices were to be of eternal duration, according to God's covenant with Levi and Judah (*Jer.xxxiii.*12–22). There would always be a Levitic priest and a Davidic king, the two Messiahs of Essene interpretation, as in the *Testaments of the XII Patriarchs*:

And now, my children, obey Levi and Judah, and be not lifted up against these two tribes, for from them shall arise unto you the salvation of God. For the Lord shall raise up from Levi as it were a high priest and from Judah as it were a king: he shall save all the race of Israel.[9]

It is otherwise an unexplained curiosity of the Messianic Hope that it envisaged two redemptive personalities, priestly and regal, answering to which there appeared almost simultaneously on the plane of history John the Baptist, son of the priest Zechariah, and Jesus, son of Joseph, of the line of David.

But just now we are in an earlier period, and concerned with the priestly figure of the True Teacher. Nevertheless it is desirable at this juncture to trace the development of the concept of the Priestly Messiah as a result of Essene doctrine.

### Chapter Six

# The Priestly Messiah

We diverge a little here to trace some of the developments of the anticipation of a Priestly Messiah to which the status and experiences of the True Teacher contributed. While with the Zadokite-Essenes the Priestly Messiah would, if anything, be the superior of the Royal Messiah, with the Pharisees the Royal Messiah would be paramount, and the Priestly Messiah no more than his precursor. The interchange of concepts moved this way and that, yet somehow it incorporated the idea of two redemptive personalities.

The first of the two has a reconciling function. Because only when Israel – or in a narrower context the Elect of Israel – should adhere to the Covenant could the final redemption take place. The mysterious language of the last prophetic book of the Old Testament, that of *Malachi* (My Messenger), sees the coming of that Messenger of the Covenant who "shall purify the sons of Levi" (*Mal*.iii.1-4), and also the return of the Prophet Elijah as reconciler (*Mal*.iv.5-6).In Messianic lore the two could be one, and that one the Priestly Messiah in the capacity of True Teacher of the Last Times.

Thus it came to be deduced that the Prophet Elijah had been a priest. He is called in the Talmud Elijah the Just, and it was accepted that he was descended from Aaron. It is related of Rava bar Abuhu that he encountered Elijah in a cemetery. "Is not my master a priest?" exclaimed the Rabbi. "Why, then, dost thou stand in a cemetery?"[1]

Even more positive is a passage in a later midrash:

To that generation [i.e. in Egypt] Thou didst send redemption through two redeemers, as it is said (*Ps*.cv.26), 'He sent Moses His servant and Aaron whom He had chosen.' And also to this generation [i.e. of the Last Times] He sendeth two, corresponding to those other two. 'Send out Thy light and thy truth' (*Ps*.xliii.3). 'Thy light', that is the Prophet Elijah of the house of Aaron, of whom it is written (*Num*.viii.2), 'the seven lamps shall throw their light in front of the lampstand.' And 'thy truth', that is Messiah ben David, as it is said (*Ps*.cxxxii.11), 'The Lord hath sworn unto David (in) truth, He will not turn from it.' And likewise it is said (*Isa*.xlii.1), 'Behold My servant whom I uphold.'[2]

Already much earlier, in the *Book of Ben Sira* in the Apocrypha, the work known as *Ecclesiasticus*,[3] Elijah is given the redemptive task "to turn the heart of the father to the son," but also "to restore the tribes of Jacob." The Messenger-Elijah figure of *Malachi* appears in another priestly guise in the *Targum of Palestine*, an interpretative Aramaic paraphrase of the Pentateuch. There it is said of the priest Phineas, the grandson of Aaron, "Behold, I confirm to him My covenant of peace, and will make him a Messenger of the Covenant, that he may ever live to announce the Redemption at the End of the Days."[4] Indeed, Phineas and Elijah are actually regarded in certain Jewish sources as one and the same person.[5] To complete the circle the medieval Jewish sect of Karaites, influenced by a much older recovery of Dead Sea Scrolls than the modern one, composed a prayer, still recited by their descendants, which petitions, "And may God send us the Teacher of Righteousness (i.e. the True Teacher) to guide the hearts of the fathers towards their children."[6]

Inevitably, with the priestly Messiah traditions, we are drawn into the Christian sphere, where Jesus identifies the priestly John the Baptist with Elijah redevivus "who comes first to restore all things" (*Mk*.ix.12). Moreover, John as Elijah is a suffering Messianic personality, as in the Joseph tradition attaching to the True Teacher. Jesus says of the Baptist, "Elijah has indeed come, and they have done to him whatever they wished, *as it is written of him*" (*Mk*.ix.13). To what document is Jesus referring?

We are made aware from Christian sources that there was a considerable Jewish sect in rivalry with the followers of Jesus, who held that John the Baptist was the true Messiah; and this position is still represented by the venerable sect of Mandaeans still surviving in southern Iraq.[7]

So strong was the expectation of a Priestly Messiah, as well as a Royal Messiah, among the Essenes and Jewish groups in contact with them, that early Christian propaganda found it essential to convey that Jesus had fulfilled both promises in his own person.

The foundation for this view was seen in the prophecy communicated to the high priest Joshua (Jesus) son of Josedech relating to the "man whose name is 'The Branch' . . . who shall rule upon his throne, and shall be a priest upon his throne" (*Zech*.vi.12-13). And more particularly the monarch in *Psalm* cx.4 is advised, "Thou art a priest for ever after the order of Melchizedek". Melchizedek was the priest-king of Salem who blessed Abraham (*Gen*.xiv.18). In accordance with these references the Maccabees, as a new dynasty of priest-kings, took the title of "Priest of the Most High God."

The Melchizedek argument is developed by the author of the *Epistle to the Hebrews,* chs.vii–x, to establish that Jesus was in fact high priest as well as king, even though he had sprung from the tribe of Judah, "of which tribe Moses spake nothing concerning priesthood" (*Heb.*vii. 14). As high priest he had made the sacrifice not with the blood of bulls and goats but with his own blood, to atone for the sins of his people. Jesus son of Joseph thus fits into the Suffering ben Joseph tradition. The same thing, and perhaps even more strongly, could be said of his brother Jacob (James), who represented him as Messianic leader for many years after he was taken away. The New Testament, in the *Acts* and Pauline Epistles, only hints at the status of Jacob, the Lord's brother. But, as we shall demonstrate later,[8] it was recognized, especially by the Judaeo-Christians, that he was a much more significant figure than the Church has appreciated.

Of Jacob it was handed down that "he was of the lineage of David . . . and moreover we have found that he officiated after the manner of the ancient priesthood. Wherefore also he was permitted once a year to enter into the Holy of Holies (i.e. on the Day of Atonement), as the Law commanded the high priests, according to that which is written; for so many before us have told of him, both Eusebius and Clement and others. Furthermore he was empowered to wear on his head the high-priestly diadem, as the aforementioned trustworthy men have attested in their memoirs."[9]

Are we to consider it purely as a coincidence that this Son of Joseph, like his brother Jesus, should have been brought to his death by a Wicked Priest?[10]

The strength of the Levitical tradition may be gauged from the Mandaean literature. The descendants of the followers of John the Baptist asserted that he was descended from Moses,[11] who of course was of the tribe of Levi. There were Christian authorities who also claimed Jesus as a Levite. Among them we find St. Ephraim the Syrian, who informs us that "when Jesus sent Peter to catch a fish in order to pay the tribute money (*Mt.*xvii.24–27) the Pharisees went with him. And when he had drawn out the fish, which had in its mouth a stater, the symbol of dominion, those haughty ones were reproved and confounded, because they believed not that he was a Levite, to whom the sea and the fishes were witnesses that he is king and priest."[12] As we shall discover, the sign of the fish, much used by the early Christians to represent their faith, was employed for Levi in a system where the signs of the zodiac corresponded with the twelve tribes of Israel.[13]

But we must also take account of the Samaritan hope of the advent of the Taheb or Shaheb, the Restorer, the Prophet like Moses. In the Samaritan Pentateuch the promise of this prophet in *Deuteronomy* is included as the Samaritan tenth Commandment.

The Taheb is not exactly the Messiah, but he is to perform Messianic functions, inaugurating the era of the return of God's favour to Israel, the *Rahuta*. He will be Prophet, Priest and King, over the "Second Kingdom." In his time will be fulfilled the promise to Phineas, whose righteous priestly seed has been kept hidden away in absolute purity and sanctity during the period of the *Fanuta* (the turning away of God's favour). The pure priests will be brought back by God to perform their office, just as the lost original Scroll of the Law will be revealed from its hiding place. The Taheb, the Perfect Man, restorer of God's favour, will come out of the desert. He will be of the tribe of Levi. His birth will be announced by the rise of a new and everlasting star in the heavens. At the same time a high priest of the line of Phineas will appear, who like Enoch had been translated to heaven; and he will serve in the new temple on Mt. Gerizim. At the age of 120 years the Taheb will die, and will be buried by the sacred mount. Over his grave the star of his advent will continue to shine.[14]

Josephus records (*Antiq.*XVIII.85-87) how a claimant to be the Taheb appeared among the Samaritans about the same time as Jesus was manifesting himself as Messiah. The Samaritans streamed towards Mt. Gerizim where this Taheb promised to reveal to them the sacred vessels of the Tabernacle which Moses had buried there. Pontius Pilate sent his troops against them and killed many, taking others prisoners who were afterwards executed.

Had it not been widely believed, on the authority of the Essene prophets and teachers, that at this period the Last Times had come there might not have arisen those who claimed to fulfill the predictions.

It can be judged, therefore, that the influence of Essene ideas on other contemporary groups among the Jews and Samaritans was considerable. We have a number of evidences of it, to some of which allusion will be made as we proceed. But what remains insufficiently accounted for is how the name of Joseph came to be linked with the Priestly Messiah, so that he should be described in later interpretations as Messiah ben Joseph. The link that we have found is that the True Teacher, like the Patriarch Joseph, had been separated from his brethren and was expected to be the means of their salvation, and that he had been a seer and a righteous man. Certainly in the Gospels Jesus is a Ben Joseph (son of Joseph), and so is his brother Jacob (James). But Rabbinical circles would be unlikely to borrow from Christianity.

In Jewish literature of the Talmudic Age the Messiah ben Joseph is represented as being the forerunner of the Messiah ben David, destined to fall in battle against the enemies of Israel. In any case in later Jewish concepts, whether in battle or simply as a martyr, he is killed by the agent of Belial, the arch-enemy of Israel, later identified as Armilus (Romulus – Rome).

The very name Joseph is one to conjure with in the Bible. And it is linked with another, namely Asaph. The former signifies to add or increase, while the latter means to collect and even to take away. The Patriarch's mother, Rachel, calls him Joseph, because God has taken away (*asaph*) her reproach of being childless and will add (*joseph*) to her another son (Joseph's brother Benjamin).[15]

The Asaph aspect takes us even deeper into the Messianic mystery linked with the True Teacher.

### Chapter Seven

# The Asaph Connection

In the Introduction to this book I pointed out how in pursuit of the identity of the True Teacher I made contact with a variety of traditions attaching to another Biblical personality, that of Asaph the Levite. This name stood revealed when I applied a venerable form of Hebrew cipher to an otherwise meaningless name in the Essenite work known as the *Assumption of Moses*. The name as it stands, TAXO, is there given to a pious Levite of the time of Antiochus Epiphanes, who retires to a cave with his seven sons. By the Atbash cipher TAXO in Hebrew letters converts to ASAPH.[1]

This disclosure of the name Asaph opened up a line of inquiry comparable with and related to that of Joseph. Here the Biblical association was with the Levite Asaph ben Berechiah of the time of King Solomon. He is presumed to have been the founder of the choral guild attached to the Temple at Jerusalem, known as the Sons of Asaph, and was himself a psalmist and singer. Already, before the close of the Old Testament canon, or at least in its final redaction, Asaph was being depicted as an individual of special significance. It is noteworthy that there is no reference to him in the Bible in the books of the *Kings*. He is mentioned, however, in the late priestly books of *Chronicles, Ezra* and *Nehemiah*. In the first of these, peculiarly, Asaph is called a seer and in the Greek LXX version a prophet (*II Chron.* xxix.30). It is conceivable that the Chasidim were responsible for this, possibly in oblique allusion to the True Teacher.

The True Teacher is described in the *Habakkuk Commentary*, among the Dead Sea Scrolls, as "the priest whom God placed in the house of Judah to explain all the words of His servants the Prophets (and expound from) the Book of God all that will befall His people Israel" (i.5). To him "God made known all the secrets of His servants the Prophets" (ii.1-3).

Certainly, in Jewish and Islamic folklore, Asaph ben Berechiah is presented as a master of occult lore, a princely figure, the confidant of King Solomon, one who knew the Ineffable Name of God, and thus had the power to perform miracles.[2] His stature became greatly magnified.

The name of Asaph is attached to twelve of the psalms in the Biblical collection, those number l and lxxiii-lxxxiii inclusive. At least two of these psalms, lxxiv and lxxxiii, have been placed by scholars in the Maccabean period, and one of them *Ps.*lxxix is directly quoted in a consequential passage in *I Maccabees*, as we have already seen. Here we give this passage in full.

And there were gathered together unto Alcimus and Bacchides a company of Scribes to seek for justice. And the Chasidim were the first among the Children of Israel that sought peace of them; for they said, 'One that is a priest of the seed of Aaron is come with the forces, and he will do us no wrong.' And he (i.e. Alcimus) spake with them words of peace, and sware unto them, saying, 'We will seek the hurt neither of you nor your friends.' And they gave him credence: and he laid hands on three-score men of them, and slew them in one day, according to the word which he wrote, 'The flesh of Thy saints (did they cast out), and their blood did they shed round about Jerusalem; and there was no man to bury them' (*I Macc.*vii.12-17).

The word which *who* wrote? Who was the author of the words quoted whom the author of *I. Maccabees* did not wish to name? The answer is Asaph, for the quotation is from *Ps.* lxxix.2-3, one of the Asaphite psalms. There are other links between these psalms and the literature of the Maccabean period.

*Ps.*lxxxiii, last of the Asaphite psalms, speaks of a confederacy against Israel, which includes Edom and Moab, Ammon and Amalek, the Philistines with the inhabitants of Tyre, and Assur. These are among the enemies of Israel prophesied against in the late section of *Jeremiah* (xxv and xlvi-li). In the war of Esau against Jacob, described in the book of *Jubilees* xxxvii, there is a similar list, which it has long been seen refers to the Syrians and their allies against whom the Maccabees fought (*I Macc.*v). The list comes up again as the Host of Belial in the apocalyptic *War of the Sons of Light with the Sons of Darkness* found among the Dead Sea Scrolls, a work which contains battle and victory hymns.

Both the *War of the Sons of Light* and the *Thanksgiving Psalms* of the Essenes have distinct points of contact with the hymns in the *Gospel of Luke* in the Nativity section, and the *Thanksgiving Psalms* are also reflected in one of the so-called *Odes of Solomon* of the early Essenite Christians. Asaph ben Berechiah lived in the reign of King Solomon, who was anointed by Zadok the Priest. It is not surprising, therefore, that collections of hymns subsequently appeared among the Pious ascribed to Solomon, and that they revered the name of Zadok.

It is significant that in the Asaph psalms in the Bible Joseph is several times used as a synonym for Israel, and that in one instance the name is written in the Hebrew as Jehoseph (*Ps*.lxxxi.5). We are reminded that the leadership of the Israelites, who settled on the east of Egypt, was attributed by the Egyptian priest Manetho to one named Osarsiph.[3] Here the name Joseph has been Egyptianised. The Jo (Greek Io) has been taken to represent the Hebrew God-name, and for this the Egyptian Osar (Osiris) has been substituted.

We may well ask how much were the present text and structure of the Hebrew Old Testament attributable to the priestly scribes of the Chasidim? It could bear their imprint in more respects than has been recognised.

During the persecution under Antiochus Epiphanes there was wholesale destruction of the sacred books, and according to the Introduction to *II Maccabees* (ii.14) it was Judas Maccabaeus who "gathered together for us all those writings that had been scattered by reason of the war that befell." Here Judas, represented as leader of the Chasidim, plays the part of Asaph as in the meaning of the name of gatherer or collector. Much work of restoration must have been necessitated, giving opportunity for the insertion of certain sections and concealed references to the contemporary situation. There is a possible hint at the activities of the Chasidim in *Jubilees* xlv.16, where it is said that Jacob bequeathed all his books, and the books of his fathers, to Levi his son, "that he might preserve them and renew them for his children *until this day*." *Jubilees* is believed to have been written about 140-130 B.C. The prolific industry and interpretative skill of the Qumran scribes offers its own confirmation; and when it comes to playing didactic games with ciphers and mysterious allusions we have to learn to play them in their way.

The Taxo-Asaph of the *Assumption of Moses* has seven sons. This puts the 'Sons of Asaph' in a special context, like the 'Sons of Zadok'. It should be noted what is said in the *Testament of Levi* (xviii): "Then shall the Lord raise up a new priest. And to him all the words of the Lord will be revealed . . . He shall give the majesty of the Lord to his sons in truth for evermore." This passage follows a reference to the Seventh Week in which there will be an apostate priesthood (xvii.11), comparable with iv and v of the *Assumption of Moses* before the advent of Taxo-Asaph.[4]

We also read in *Enoch* xciii.9–10, "And after this in the Seventh Week will a generation rise and many will be its deeds, and all its deeds will be apostate. And at its close will the Elect of Righteousness of the Eternal Plant of Righteousness be elected to receive the *sevenfold* instruction of His whole creation."

We should not expect from the Essene and cognate literature too much in the way of straightforward and clear cut references to known persons and events. And this in part is due, especially as regards the chief protagonists, to their representation of the opposing cosmic forces, the True Teacher on one side and the Wicked Priest on the other. In this respect they are types, as well as having a reference to particular historical individuals, in the clash at the End of the Days between the forces of Good and Evil. Sometimes the types are related to Old Testament characters, such as Joseph and Asaph, which could be considered peculiarly relevant and employed to protect the real identity of the True Teacher. And sometimes there are allusions to various personalities, as already described in chapters iii and iv above, who were contemporaries or near-contemporaries at the crucial period in the second century B.C.

All this rather complicates obtaining a clear picture of the actual True Teacher. This does not mean that he was non-existent, and from the Essene records we are able to learn a considerable amount about him. The Asaph aspect itself is very pertinent, for it acquaints us with a man of the priestly tribe who is both a prophet and a seer, and who notably expressed his faith, as well as his tribulations, in psalms and songs.

Among the earliest of the Dead Sea Scrolls to be recovered in modern times were the so-called *Thanksgiving Psalms*. They were given this initial title because so many of them opened with the words, "I thank Thee, O Lord." Scholars were not slow to observe that some of these psalms, notably numbers 1 and 2, and numbers 7-11 inclusive, appeared to be autobiographical, reflecting, as one translator of the Scrolls expressed it, "the experiences of a teacher abandoned by his friends and persecuted by his enemies."[5] Various authorities, such as Dupont-Sommer, accordingly attributed the whole collection to the True Teacher.

And this was not the first find of Essene psalm-collections. In a letter written in 819 A.D. by Timotheus, Metropolitan of Seleucia, he relates that "Jews from Jerusalem, seeking admission to the Church, had told him that about ten years previously a cave was discovered near Jericho containing a hoard of Hebrew manuscripts of the Bible and other writings and that these manuscripts were taken by the Jews to Jerusalem." Among them were no less than 200 non-Biblical psalms, called by Timotheus "Psalms of David." This does not necessarily mean that they were ascribed to that monarch.[6] These psalms will have formed part of the ancient Essene collection. Here from the *Thanksgiving Psalms*, as translated by Vermes, we give some typical and significant extracts.

### From Psalm 1

I have been a byword to traitors,
    the assembly of the wicked has raged against me;
they have roared like turbulent seas,
    and their towering waves have spat out mud and slime.
But to the elect of righteousness
    Thou hast made me a banner,
and a discerning interpreter of wonderful mysteries,
    to try (those who practice) truth
and to test those who love correction.

### From Psalm 2

Violent men have sought after my life
    because I have clung to Thy Covenant.
For they, an assembly of deceit,
    and a horde of Satan,
know not that my stand
    is maintained by Thee,
And that in Thy mercy Thou wilt save my soul,
    since my steps proceed from Thee.
From Thee it is
    that they assail my life,
that Thou mayest be glorified
    by the judgement of the wicked,
and manifest Thy might through me
    in the presence of the sons of men;
for it is by Thy mercy that I stand.

### From Psalm 7

Teachers of lies (have smoothed) Thy people (with words),
    and (false prophets) have led them astray;
they perish without understanding
    for their words are in folly.
For I am despised by them
    and they have no esteem for me
that Thou mayest manifest Thy might through me.
    They have banished me from my land
like a bird from its nest;

all my friends and brethren are driven far from me,
and hold me for a broken vessel.

*From Psalm 11*

For) Thou hast succoured my soul, O my God,
    and hast lifted my horn on high.
And I shall shine in a seven-fold light
    in (the Council appointed by) Thee for Thy glory;
for Thou art an everlasting heavenly light to me
    and will establish my feet
(upon level ground for ever).

These are elevated sentiments of a man of deep faith, and are extremely moving. We can understand therefore that the True Teacher is brought before us as Psalmist and Prophet under the name Asaph. We shall now illustrate how under the same name he comes also before as Physician, a profession which in ancient times had associations with astronomy and astrology. Under this aspect we discover a very positive link with the Essenes.

*Chapter Eight*

# The Legacy of Shem

In his description of the Essenes the Jewish historian Josephus drew particular attention to their prophetic and healing powers, acquired from knowledge in sacred books which they had inherited. He writes: "They display an extraordinary interest in the writings of the ancients, singling out in particular those which make for the welfare of soul and body. With the help of these, and with a view to the treatment of diseases, they make investigations into medicinal roots and the properties of stones" (*Jewish War* II. 136). And again, "There are some among them who profess to foretell the future, being versed from their early years in holy books, various forms of purifications and apophthegms of prophets; and seldom, if ever, do they err in their predictions" (II. 159).[1]

Since the discovery of the Dead Sea Scrolls and our great familiarity with cognate literature we are in a position to confirm the statements of Josephus. In one work, the origins of which are unknown, and variously entitled *Sefer Asaf, Midrash Refu'ot*, and *Sefer Refu'ot*, the foundations of medicine are ascribed to Shem the son of Noah,[2] and the treatise itself is variously attributed to Asaph the Younger, Asaph the Sage, Asaph the Physician, and even Asaph ben Berechiah the Astronomer. This work is in Hebrew. Again the name Asaph comes positively before us, a matter that we shall pursue. But here we must again cite the famed *Book of Jubilees* from the second century B.C., which describes the ancient transmission of medical knowledge.

"And we explained to Noah all the medicines of their diseases, together with their seductions, how he might heal them with the herbs of the earth. And Noah wrote down all things in a book as we instructed him concerning every kind of medicine" (x. 12-13). All that Noah wrote he gave to his son Shem (x. 14), and in due course the ancient scripts were handed on by Jacob to Levi: "And he (Jacob) gave all his books and the books of his fathers to Levi his son that he might preserve them and renew them for his children until this day" (xlv. 16).

The *Book of Noah* can be traced back to Chasidic times, the second half of the second century B.C., and one of its instructions prohibited the eating of blood, one of the Laws of Noah imposed upon Gentile converts to Christianity (*Acts* xv.29). I am not able to cite an antique *Book of Shem*, but a late Syriac manuscript in the John Rylands Library in Manchester[3] offers a *Discourse written by Shem son of Noah concerning the beginning of the year and all that happens in it*. This might be described as Old Shem's Almanac. The text itself goes back to the Roman period and of particular interest is the author's concern for the area of Damascus and the Hauran, which may have Essene associations.[4]

Forming part of the same manuscript it is significant to find another work having reference to Asaph. This consists of an extract from a Greek writer called 'Andronicus the Wise, the Philosopher, and the Learned.' Mingana believed it probable that the author in question was Andronicus Cyrrhestes, who was a contemporary of the early Chasidim, and who is credited by Vetruvius (1,6.4) with the setting up of the octagonal marble tower at Athens, now commonly known as the Temple of the Winds. According to Andronicus, "Asaph the writer and historian of the Hebrews explains and teaches clearly the history of all these (i.e. the signs of the zodiac), but does not show them with Greek names, but according to the sons of Jacob . . . He begins then in the Aramaic language and puts at the head Taurus, which he calls 'Reuben'." In view of the early Christian employment of the symbol of the fish we observe with special interest in the list the identification of Pisces with Levi.[5]

Asaph is here described as a Jewish writer and historian; but this description may be due to the Syriac translator from the original Aramaic, who conceivably confused Asaph with Joseph, and identified him with the well-known historian Josephus. The Joseph-Asaph conjunction is one which we have already observed, and of which we shall learn much more later.[6]

We return here to the *Book of Medicines (Sefer Refu'ot)*, a Hebrew document in varying recensions associated with the name of Asaph, with which scholars have long been familiar. In recent times the language of this work has been found to have points of contact with expressions in the Dead Sea Scrolls; and the book may well have been Essene in origin. An interesting aspect is its inclusion of a pact or covenant between Asaph with his colleague Yochanan ben Zabda and their pupils on lines which suggest a deliberately created Jewish version of the Pythagorean Hippocratic Oath. An extract from the text reads as follows:

(47) You shall not incline after lucre (so as) to help a godless (man in shedding) innocent blood. (48) You shall not mix a deadly drug for any man or woman so that he (or she) should kill their fellow-man. (49) You shall not speak of the herbs (out of which such drugs are made). You shall not hand them over to any man, (50) And you shall not talk about any matter (connected) with this. (51) You shall not use blood in any work of medicine.

Shlomo Pines in his erudite paper on which my references are based[7] sees a connection with the early Christian *Doctrine of the Two Ways* in the *Didache*, or *Teaching of the Twelve Apostles to the Nations*, possibly of the late first century A.D., which is also laid under tribute in the later *Apostolic Constitutions*. There each of the Apostles in turn makes his contribution, the first being John the son of Zebedee. Here, conceivably, may be a clue to how this name in its Hebrew form, Yochanan ben Zabda, got into the *Sefer Refuot* as colleague of Asaph ben Berechiah. Of course this is only a guess by Pines, and there could be a much more pertinent reason.

It could be that in the original text another John, not the Apostle, was intended. It was a common Jewish name, and Josephus for example mentions that among the Jewish commanders in the revolt against the Romans was a John the Essene. We have also to take into account that Christian tradition confused John the son of Zebedee with the Essenite John of priestly status, who appears in the New Testament as the Beloved Disciple of the Fourth Gospel, and perhaps as the author of the *Book of Revelation*, who died at a great age at Ephesus. It was his house at Jerusalem where the Last Supper was held, and which became the home of the mother of Jesus and the initial meeting place of the followers of Jesus. The *Gospel of John* furnishes this information. It also reports that at the interrogation of Jesus it was the Beloved Disciple who knew the high priest who was able to get Peter into the palace courtyard. It confirms this John's priestly status, that when he and Peter went to the tomb of Jesus he would not enter the tomb until he knew there was no corpse there. Otherwise, as a priest, he could be defiled. It is the Beloved Disciple's personal testimony that furnishes these added details.[8] It is possible that traditions about him contributed to the medieval legend of Prester John.

Whatever may be the solution to this puzzle, it is of a piece with the evidences we continually encounter of early Christian links with the Essenes. The Essenes of Josephus are skilled in the use of medicaments, and the Essenite community in Egypt described by

Philo[9] bore the name of Therapeuts, though perhaps more in relation to their piety than to medical skill. We know from the New Testament of the healing activities of the early Christians. But we also have evidence from Rabbinical and Orthodox Christian sources of Judaeo-Christians practising the Essene arts, of which we may give some instances.

A man shall have no dealings with the heretics, nor be cured by them, even for the sake of an hour of life. There was the case of Ben Dama nephew of R.Ishmael, whom a serpent bit. There came Jacob the heretic of the village of Sechanya to cure him (in the name of Jeshu ben Pandera (i.e. Jesus) *var.leg.*); but R.Ishmael would not allow him. Ben Dama said to him, 'R.Ishmael, my brother, do allow him, that I may be cured, and I will produce a text from the Torah to prove that it is permitted.' But hardly had he finished his discourse when his soul departed, and he died.[10]

The grandson of R.Joshua ben Levi had something stuck in his throat. There came a man and whispered to him in the name of Jesus, and he recovered. When the healer came out, R.Joshua, said to him, 'What was it you whispered to him?' He said to him, 'A certain word.' R.Joshua replied 'It had been better for him that he had died rather than that.'[11]

These quotations are from the *Talmud*, but much earlier in the *Mishnah* from the second century A.D. we find something similar.

R. Akiba said, 'He who reads in external (i.e. uncanonical) books, and he who whispers over a wound, and says, None of the diseases which I sent on Egypt will I lay on thee: I am the Lord thy healer (*Exod.*xv.26), has any share in the world to come.'[12]

McNeile well explained this passage. The quotation from *Exodus* in Hebrew has the numerical value of the name Jesus, and would be employed by crypto-Christians as a substitute, when they dared not pronounce the name of Jesus openly.[13]

Contemporary with the Talmudic Age (fourth century A.D.) we have some confirmation in the writings of Bishop Epiphanius, himself of Jewish origin. He tells us that he was informed by Count Joseph, a convert from Judaism, that before his conversion, when lying dangerously ill, one of the Jewish elders, a student of the Law, whispered in his ear, "Believe that Jesus the son of God was crucified under Pontius Pilate, and that he will come again to judge the living and the dead." This kind of thing was of frequent occurrence, writes the Bishop of Constantia, and mentions another Jew, who told him that once when he was on the point of death he heard a whisper in his ear from one of those who stood by, that "Jesus Christ who was crucified, the son of God, will hereafter judge thee."[14]

We cannot be sure that the words whispered were as quoted. Epiphanius may well have assimilated them to a more orthodox Christian formula. But the crypto-Christian practices are here supported.

Reverting to our other sources which we have cited there is considerable probability that both the *Book of Shem* and the *Book of Medicines* in the name of Asaph originated in the region of the Hauran around the ninth or tenth century A.D. And it is certainly conceivable that their appearance owed something to the find of Essene literature near Jericho at the beginning of the ninth century. Both documents relate to the 'Shem son of Noah' medieval traditions. And incidentally the *Book of Medicines* laid under tribute "the books of the wise men of India."

### Chapter Nine

# Son of Berechiah

We have now to turn to another aspect of the Joseph-Asaph traditions. Of the singer Asaph we are told in the Bible (*I Chron.* vi.39–43) that he was a descendant of Gershom the son of Levi, and that his father's name was Berechiah. This circumstance could be used to tie in with the True Teacher's believed martyrdom under the aspect of the priestly sufferer. Thus in Matthew's Gospel Jesus is made to say, or quote:

> Behold, I sent unto you prophets and wise men and scribes;
> And some of them ye shall kill and crucify . . . and persecute . . .
> That upon you may come all the righteous blood shed upon earth,
> From the blood of Abel the Righteous
> Unto the blood of Zechariah son of Berechiah,
> Whom ye slew between the temple and the altar.[1]

Here we meet with what appears to be a curious and significant blunder, since the Zechariah referred to was not the son of Berechiah, but the son of the priest Jehoiada who lived in the reign of King Joash. The name given in *Matthew* was corrected in the *Gospel of the Hebrews*. The reference is to *II Chronicles* xxiv.18–21:

> And they left the house of the Lord God of their fathers, and served groves and idols: and wrath came upon Judah and Jerusalem for this their trespass. Yet He sent prophets to them to bring them again unto the Lord; and they testified against them; but they would not give ear. And the Spirit of God came upon Zechariah the son of Jehoiada the priest, which stood above the people, and said unto them, 'Thus saith God, why transgress ye the commandments of the Lord, that ye cannot prosper? Because ye have forsaken the Lord, he hath also forsaken you.' And they conspired against him, and stoned him with stones at the commandment of the king, in the court of the house of the Lord.

We do find in the Bible a Zechariah son of Berechiah, a priest and prophet, who lived much later at the time of the return from the Babylonian Exile (*Zech.*i.1; *Neh.*xii.16). But there is no evidence to suggest that he suffered martyrdom. Further, we learn from Josephus of a rich man, not a priest, contemporary with himself, named

Zechariah son of Baris (or Bariscaeus), who was murdered in the Temple by the Zealots after a mock trial in 68 A.D.[2] It is conceivable that Josephus composed this incident himself out of hatred of the militant Zealots, utilising the now established Ben Berechiah legend. The legend, as we shall see, was taken over by the Church, in all probability from a Baptist source, in relation to John's father Zechariah, who in one text at least is called Son of Berechiah.

The legend was also known to the later Rabbis, and it is found in the 4th-5th century Palestinian and Babylonian Talmuds.[3] Here Zechariah is a priest, a prophet, and a judge, in the Essene tradition relating to the True Teacher, who is murdered in the Temple, and whose fate brought about the destruction of Jerusalem and the Babylonian Captivity in the time of Nebuchadnezzar. We quote the text in full.

R.Jochanan said, 'Eighty thousand priests were killed for the blood of Zechariah.' R.Juda asked R.Acha, 'Whereabouts did they kill Zechariah, in the Court of the Women, or in the Court of Israel?' He answered, 'Neither in the Court of Israel, nor in the Court of the Women, but in the Court of the Priests.[4] And it was not done to his blood as is done to the blood of a ram or a kid. Concerning the latter it is written, 'And he shall pour out its blood and cover it with dust.' But concerning the former it is written, 'Her blood is in the midst of her; she set it upon the top of a rock, she poured it not upon the ground.' And wherefore? 'That it might cause fury to come up to take vengeance.'

They committed seven wickednesses in that day. They killed a Priest, a Prophet, and a Judge; they shed the blood of an innocent man; they polluted the Court (i.e. of the Temple); and that day was the Sabbath, and the Day of Atonement. When, therefore, Nebuzzaradan (i.e. Nebuchadnezzar's general) went up thither, he saw the blood bubbling. So he said to them, 'What meaneth this?' They said, 'It is the blood of calves, lambs and rams, which we have offered on the altar.' Said he, 'Bring then calves, lambs and rams, that I may try whether this is their blood.' They brought them and slew them, but that blood still bubbled, while their blood did not bubble. 'Declare unto me this matter,' said he, 'or I will tear your flesh with iron rakes.' Then said they unto him, 'This was a Priest, a Prophet, and a Judge, who foretold to Israel all these evils which we have suffered from you; and we rose up against him, and slew him.' Said he, 'But I will appease him.' He brought the rabbis, and slew them upon that blood; and yet it was not pacified: he brought the children out of the school, and slew them upon it, and yet it was not quiet: he brought the young priests, and slew them upon it, and yet it was not quiet. So that he slew upon it ninety-four thousand, and yet it was not quiet. He drew near to it himself, and said, 'O Zechariah, Zechariah, thou hast destroyed the best of thy people; would you have me destroy all of them?' Then it was quiet, and bubbled no more.

This developed form of the legend has parallels in Christian sources, where it is reflected in accounts of the asserted martyrdom of Zechariah father of John the Baptist. In the *Gospel Commentaries* of S.Ephraim the Syrian (c.373 A.D) we read: "others say, that Zechariah, when his son was demanded of him during the slaughter of the infants (i.e. in Bethlehem, *Mt*.ii.16), because he had preserved him by flight into the desert, was slain before the altar, as the Lord said" (*Mt*.xxiii. 34-35). Early Christian sources told how Elizabeth, mother of John the Baptist, urged by her husband Zechariah, fled from Bethlehem into the wilderness with her infant son because the soldiers of King Herod were seeking to slay the Messiah who had been born (cp.*Mt*.ii and *Rev*.xii).

There is a definite parallel to the Talmudic story in the *Life of John the Baptist*, composed by Serapion, an Egyptian bishop, c.385-395 A.D. The relevant passage reads:

Let us now proceed to commemorate the holy Zecharias, the martyr, and relate to you a few of his numerous merits. I should wish to praise your true life, but I fear to hear reproof from you, similar to that you made to the blessed Elizabeth. I am full of admiration for you, O pious Zecharias! In the time when the soldiers of Herod came to you and asked you, saying, 'Where is your infant son, the child of your old age?' You did not deny the fact and say, 'I have no knowledge of such a child.' You simply answered, 'His mother took him into the desert.' And when Zecharias uttered these words to the soldiers concerning his son, they killed him inside the Temple. Then the priests shrouded his body and placed it near that of his father Berechiah in a hidden cemetery, from fear of the wicked (king); and his blood boiled on the earth for fifty years, until Titus son of Vespasian, the Emperor of the Romans, came and destroyed Jerusalem and killed the Jewish priests for the blood of Zecharias, as the Lord ordered him.[5]

The legend of the bubbling or boiling blood of the last martyr at the End-Time seems to reflect the fate of the first Just One, Abel, referred to by Jesus, in an interpretation based on *Gen*.iv.10, where God says to Cain, "The voice of thy brother's blood crieth unto Me from the ground."

Zechariah as priest, prophet and judge really represents the martyred True Teacher of the Essenes, who has already come before us in the guise of Asaph. In the Bible Asaph son of Berechiah is a prophet, and there is also the prophet Zechariah son of Berechiah, who as we have seen was made to reflect the fate of the priest Zechariah son of Jehoiada. We note that Serapion makes the father of John the Baptist to have been a Zechariah son of Berechiah.

What is emphasised in these teachings relating to the Just One is that the Great Crime inevitably brings the retribution of the Great Catastrophe. The punitive agent is a Nebuchadnezzar, an Antiochus Epiphanes, or Vespasian. The teaching finds a place in *Psalm* xciv:

> O God, to whom vengeance belongeth, shine forth.
> Lift up Thyself, Thou Judge of the earth:
> Render a reward to the proud.
> Lord, how long shall the wicked triumph? . . .
> Yet they say, The Lord shall not see,
> Neither shall the God of Jacob regard it . . .
> They gather themselves together against the soul of the Just,
> And condemn the innocent blood.
> But the Lord is my defence;
> And my God is the rock of my refuge.
> And He shall bring upon them their own iniquity,
> And shall cut them off in their own wickedness;
> Yea, the Lord our God shall cut them off."

In the *Seder Olam*, xxx (ed.Neubauer), as also in the Talmud, it is stated that this psalm was being sung by the Levites on the day the Temple was destroyed by the Romans in 70 A.D.

We shall return to this aspect of the teachings in the next chapter. But here we must draw attention to the outcome of the Essene ideas of the True Teacher and of the two Messiahs, the priestly and the regal. It was to these ideas that John the Baptist and Jesus had responded at the time indicated by the Essenes as the End Time, and after their deaths they became the cause of bitter rivalry between their respective followers. The Judaeo-Christians, who had strong links with the views of the Pharisees as well as with those of the Essenes, needed the witness of the Baptist as the priestly Elijah, forerunner of the one Messiah, the son of David. They could not therefore disparage the Baptist, and had to contrive instead to emphasise his secondary place. This is brought out strongly in the Gospels, and particularly emphasised in the Fourth Gospel:

John (The Baptist) answered and said . . . 'Ye yourselves bear me witness that I said, I am not the Messiah, but that I am sent before him. He that hath the bride is the bridegroom: but the friend of the bridegroom, which standeth and heareth him, rejoiceth greatly because of the bridegroom's voice: this my joy therefore is fulfilled. He must increase, but I must decrease (*Jn*.iii.27-30).

Contact with followers of John the Baptist, indicated in the *Acts of the Apostles* (xviii.24-26, xix.1-5), acquainted the Christians with the

Nativity stories of John in which he figured as the infant Messiah of the priestly traditions, born at Bethlehem. Access to the literature of the still surviving Baptist sect of Mandaeans in Iraq, as well as early Christian sources, enables us to reconstruct this material at least in outline.[6]

The priest Zechariah has a vision that a son will be born to him and his wife Elizabeth who will be the salvation of Israel. His birth will be miraculous as Elizabeth is past child-bearing age. The child is born in Bethlehem, as the incarnation of the heavenly Man of Essene tradition. According to the Mandaean texts "he was planted out of the heights and laid in Elizabeth's womb." After his birth Magi come from the East to Jerusalem seeking the Messiah whose star they have seen, and are directed by King Herod to Bethlehem, where they pay homage to the infant John. Zechariah is warned by an angel that Herod will seek to kill the child, and sends Elizabeth away with her son John into the wilderness. The infants in Bethlehem are massacred, but John has escaped. Zechariah is interrogated in the Temple, and murdered, according to one line of tradition. But Mandaean sources exclude this. They hold that both Zechariah and Elizabeth lived on, while John was preserved in the wilderness. When the time came for him to begin his mission he was brought back on a cloud to Jerusalem, much to the astonishment of his now aged parents.

The indications are that the authors of the Gospels of *Matthew* and *Luke* used the Baptist material in different ways in the interest of the Messiahship of Jesus. Thus *Matthew* takes over the Magi incident and the massacre of the infants at Bethlehem, while Luke incorporates the account of the birth of John while subordinating his status to that of Jesus and omitting the Magi incident and its sequel. It is the Baptist Nativity legends which help to explain the conflicting accounts of the birth of Jesus.

### Chapter Ten

# My Servant Jacob

So strong were the Essene teachings about the End-Time personalities that they were seen to find fulfilment not only in John the Baptist and Jesus, on the side of the forces of Light, but also especially in Jacob (James) son of Joseph and a younger brother of Jesus. By general assent he became head of the followers of Jesus, a kind of regent for the temporarily absent king, with his seat at Jerusalem. Tradition claimed, as we have already seen,[1] that he officiated in the Temple in the capacity of high priest, thus combining both Messianic functions. It is likely, however, that this belief arose because the high priest was president of the Sanhedrin, and Jacob acted in the same capacity as head of the Nazorean Sanhedrin. In the *Epistle of Clement to James*, which prefaces the *Clementine Homilies*, he is addressed as: "The Lord and Bishop of Bishops, who rules Jerusalem, the holy church of the Hebrews, and the churches everywhere founded by the providence of God."

The eminence and significance of Jacob as the Messiah's brother finds many references in the ancient records, but is suppressed in Catholic doctrine, so that laymen and even many clergy are denied information about it. In the *Gospel of Thomas*, recovered not long ago from Egypt, we read in one passage:

> The disciples said to Jesus:
> > We know that you will go away from us,
> > Who will be great over us?
> Jesus said to them:
> > In the place to which you have gone (i.e. Jerusalem),
> > you will go to James the Just,
> > for whose sake the heaven and the earth
> > > came into existence.[2]

In the *Gospel of the Hebrews* Jesus makes his first appearance after the resurrection to his brother Jacob.[3] Tradition claims that he followed an ascetic way of life in the fashion of the Essenes, and even stricter. He was said to have been a Nazirite from birth. Testimony to this effect had been given in the second century by the Christian historian Hegesippus in the Fifth Book of his *Memoirs*. He is quoted as stating:

Now Jacob, the brother of the Lord, who, as there were many of that name, was termed the Just by all, from the days of our Lord until now, received the government of the Church with the apostles. This apostle was consecrated (to God) from his mother's womb. He drank neither wine nor fermented liquors, and abstained from animal food. A razor never came upon his head; he never anointed himself with oil, neither did he bathe. He alone was allowed to enter the Holy Place. He never wore woollen, only linen garments. He was in the habit of entering the Temple alone, and was often to be found upon his knees and interceding for the forgiveness of the people; so that his knees became as hard as a camel's . . . And indeed on account of his exceeding great piety, he was called the Just (i.e. *Zaddik*) and Oblias (i.e. *Ophla-am*), which signifies Justice and the People's Bulwark; as the Prophets declare concerning him.[4]

It is significant that Jacob should be deemed of such consequence that he had been the subject of prophecy. The predictions are not cited, but might relate to the interpretation of *Isaiah*, chapters xlii ff, where reference is made to "My servant Jacob". On the other hand, what could have been in mind were the Messianic predictions of the Essenes in their literature relating to the Priestly Sufferer.

Like the True Teacher of the Essenes the brother of Jesus was brought to his death by a Wicked Priest, the high priest Annas or Ananus, in 62 A.D. The circumstances are related by Josephus:

Possessed of such a character (i.e. for rashness and daring) Ananus thought that he had a favourable opportunity because Festus was dead and Albinus was still on the way. And so he convened the judges of the Sanhedrin and brought before them a man named Jacob, the brother of Jesus who was called the Christ, and certain others. He accused them of having transgressed the Law and delivered them up to be stoned. Those of the inhabitants of the city (i.e. Jerusalem) who were considered the most fair-minded and who were strict in the observance of the Law[5] were offended at this. They therefore secretly sent to King Agrippa urging him, for Ananus had not even been correct in his first step (i.e. convening the Sanhedrin without official sanction), to order him to desist from any further such actions. Certain of them even went to meet Albinus, who was on his way from Alexandria, and informed him that Ananus had no authority to convene the Sanhedrin without his consent. Convinced by these words, Albinus angrily wrote to Ananus threatening to take vengeance upon him. King Agrippa, because of Ananus' action deposed him from the high priesthood, which he had held for three months.[6]

A somewhat different and less reliable version of Jacob's death was given considerably later by Hegesippus, though both agree that he was stoned. We quote the concluding sentence as this is of special interest. "Thus he (Jacob) suffered martyrdom, and they buried him on the spot where his tombstone still remains, close to the Temple. He became a faithful witness, both to the Jews and Greeks, that Jesus is the Christ. Immediately after this, Vespasian invaded and took Judaea."[7]

Here we cannot fail to perceive the likeness to the Zechariah saga. Not only is the victim killed in proximity to the Temple, but also the event is followed by the Roman invasion under Vespasian. The latter circumstance would seem to imply that Vespasian's action was a punishment for the killing of the saint.

And this is borne out by a statement made by the Church Father Origen in the third century. He alludes to a passage in Josephus not now extant, which may have appeared in the *Jewish War*, as some scholars have held. But it is a possibility that Origen may have confused Hegesippus with Josephus due to the similarity of the names. What had surprised him was that Jacob had been made more important than his brother Jesus, since the fall of Jerusalem was treated as a punishment for the death of the former rather than the latter. We give Origen's own words:

Although not believing in Jesus as the Christ (i.e. Messiah), Josephus, when searching for the true cause of the fall of Jerusalem, ought to have said that the persecution of Jesus was the cause of its ruin, because the people had killed the prophesied Messiah. Yet, as if against his will and not far from the truth, he says that this befell the Jews in revenge for Jacob the Just, who was the brother of Jesus the so-called Christ, because they killed him, although he was a perfectly just man.[8]

When we consider how John the Baptist, Jesus and his brother Jacob, are represented in the traditions, we can appreciate how strong was the Essene impact on the Messianic concepts of the first century A.D. They had developed in the preceding century and a half, having owed much to the experience of the True Teacher, and the veneration in which he came to be held. The expectation of the royal Messiah of the line of David, espoused by the Pharisees, made a strong appeal to the Jewish masses. But the Essenes had placed squarely beside it the doctrine of the suffering priestly Messiah, which no less had to find fulfilment.

The Messianic positions occupied by the Judaeo-Christians and Baptists are in their way a testimony to the historicity of the True

Teacher and to the beliefs to which his activities gave rise.

It may be well to put in a word here about the ancient historians and biographers, including the authors of the canonical Gospels. Their practices were very different from what would now be held to be legitimate. They would compose speeches for their characters, where these were not available, in terms deemed appropriate to the individual and the circumstances. And sometimes, in the interest of propaganda, they would credit such characters with sentiments favoured by the writer, but which indeed might be quite alien to the person to whom they were attributed. Where information was lacking, or where the author found in the records of other personalities incidents which would be appropriate for his hero, or enhance his reputation, he did not hesitate to take these over. The author did not regard this as fraudulent. Similarly supernatural incidents would be introduced or individuals credited with special powers.

We have to keep these techniques continually in mind as we assess the records which are being brought to our attention. What the ancients thought desirable was a telling, rich and entertaining narrative with an elevated tone. This might involve suitable borrowing, but such transference was thought to be allowable and not as creating a fiction. It is due to ignoring all such factors that some rationalist writers have concluded, for example, that Jesus never existed.

*Chapter Eleven*

# Jeremiah The Prophet

The developments as regards New Testament personalities are among the best evidences we have that the True Teacher really existed, and they also witness to his position of eminence. But with the aid of the Dead Sea Scrolls it has become more practicable to place him in the setting of his own period. That period, as indicated by our inquiries, was around the second half of the second century B.C. It is perhaps unfortunate that we do not know as yet, and perhaps never will know, the Teacher's real name or very much of his life story. But we are able now to speak more positively about his experiences, as we have already illustrated, and the effects of his teaching.

In our pursuit of information we encounter the significance of the Prophet Jeremiah for the True Teacher and his followers, and also for the Chasidim. This prophet, believed to be of priestly family, who preached and suffered at the time of the capture of Jerusalem by the Babylonians, is suddenly in the Maccabaean period given a place of special prominence. Let us consider here some of the evidence.

The Prophet Jeremiah had spoken of a New Covenant which God would make with His repentant people (*Jer*.xxxi. 31-31).[1] This promise was taken up by the Chasidim of the Seleucid period, as we find in the Dead Sea Scrolls. At a certain time in the 'Period of the Wrath' a body of them emigrated from Israel to the Land of the North, where under instruction of the Lawgiver, or Student of the Law, they entered into a New Covenant.[2] One cannot be positive that the True Teacher and the Student of the Law were one and the same person; but this seems most likely.

It was Jeremiah also who had spoken of God's perpetual covenant with the Levitical Priesthood, as well as with the House of David (*Jer*.xxxiii. 17-22). Again, in the context of these passages, we find Jeremiah buying a piece of ground, and, in the hearing of those Jews who were with him in prison, instructing his disciple Baruch to have the purchase documents put "in an earthen vessel, that they may continue many days (xxxii. 14)". This was to be a sign from God that "fields shall be bought in this land, whereof ye say, It is desolate, without man or beast; it is given into the hands of the Chaldeans" (43).

In the same prophetic vein the Essenes deposited their sacred books in caves in sealed earthenware jars. They speak of an instruction by the Lawgiver (in this case Moses) to Joshua his successor, to preserve certain special books by anointing them with cedar oil and putting them away in earthen vessels "until the date of repentance in the visitation wherewith the Lord shall visit them in the Consummation at the End of the Days" (*Assumption of Moses*, ii. 16–17).

There is another Jeremiah tradition in *II Macc.*ii. 1–8. Here the prophet "being warned of God, commanded that the Tabernacle and the Ark (i.e. of the Covenant) should follow with him, when he went forth into the mountain where Moses went up and beheld the heritage of God." The text then continues:

And Jeremiah came and found a cavern in the rock, and there he brought in the Tabernacle, and the Ark, and the altar of incense; and he made fast the entrance. And some of those who followed with him came there that they might mark the way, and they could not find it. But when Jeremiah perceived this, he blamed them, saying, 'Yea, and the place shall be unknown until God gather the people again together, and mercy come; and then shall the Lord disclose these things.'[3]

In keeping with this tradition the Samaritans held the belief that in the last Days there would come the Restorer (*Taheb*) of the line of Aaron, who would recover the original vessels of the Tabernacle in the Wilderness from their original hiding place. John the Baptist and Jesus, as we have observed, appeared at what the Essenes claimed were the Last Times, and similarly in the same period one who believed he was the Taheb.

The special significance of the Prophet Jeremiah for the Chasidim and their successors is further illustrated by the author of the Essenite *II Maccabees*. In chapter xv. 12–16 he reports a dream of Judas Maccabaeus.

And the vision of that dream was this: he saw Onias, him that was formerly high priest, a noble and good man, reverend in bearing ... with outstretched hands invoking blessings on the whole body of the Jews: thereupon he saw a man appear, of venerable age and exceeding glory, and wonderful and most majestic was the dignity around him. And Onias answered and said, 'This is the lover of the brethren, he who prayeth much for the people and the holy city, Jeremiah the prophet of God.' And Jeremiah stretching forth his hand delivered to Judas a sword of gold, and in giving it addressed him thus, 'Take the holy sword, a gift from God, wherewith thou shalt smite down the adversaries.'

There would seem to be little doubt that the Chasidim's comparison of their own time, considered as a second judgement on Israel, with the time of Nebuchadnezzar's conquest, the first, promoted a special interest in the Prophet Jeremiah, and led to the production of apocryphal books in his name and that of his disciple Baruch. This was to happen again after the destruction of Jerusalem by the Romans in A.D.70.

But we come now to a mysterious aspect of the *Book of Jeremiah* in the Bible – the employment in it of the *Atbash* cipher, the cipher which we have seen employed in the Dead Sea Scrolls and in the Essenite *Assumption of Moses*, and which disclosed the name of Asaph.[5] Very few readers of the Bible are aware of this significant circumstance.

I drew attention to the evidence when I was working on the Dead Sea Scrolls not long after their recovery, and cannot do better than repeat here what I wrote as far back as 1955,[6] and somewhat amplify the details.

The *Atbash* cipher is used four times in the *Book of Jeremiah*, twice in chapter xxv and twice in chapter li. In xxv the Prophet is told to take the wine cup of fury and make all nations drink it. The list includes the Philistines, Edom and Moab, and the Children of Ammon, and in verse 2 we have, "And all the kings of Zimri, and all the kings of Elam." It has long been agreed that Zimri should be read as Zimchi (זמכי), which by the cipher converts into Elam (עילם). This is confirmed by the parallel passage in the Greek *Septuagint* version, which speaks only of Elam and omits Zimri or Zimchi altogether. At the end of the list in the following verse we read, "And the king of Sheshach shall drink after them. Sheshach (ששך) by the cipher becomes Babel (בבל), namely Babylon. The whole clause is omitted in the Greek version of *Jeremiah*. Sheshach is again mentioned alongside Babel (Babylon) in chapter li.41, where again the parallel passage in the Greek omits the Sheshach clause.

In the first verse of the same chapter there is another example of *Atbash*. We read: "Behold I will raise up against Babylon, and against them that dwell *lev-kamai*, a destroying wind." The difficult Hebrew words quoted are converted by the cipher into *Kasdim* (Chaldeans), and the Greek parallel plainly says, "and against the Chaldeans dwelling therein." The Greek translator, therefore, had knowledge of the cipher being used in the Hebrew, and simply left out the clauses containing it where conversion involved a duplication of names, or, as in the last instance, converted the cipher words where no duplication was involved. Because of the cipher it does become important to ask, what was the date of these chapters in which it occurs?

In the Hebrew text of *Jeremiah* a wide gulf separates chapter xxv from chapter li. But in the Greek version this is not so. In the latter there is a radical difference in the arrangement of the later chapters. The group of chapters xlvi-li in the Hebrew is broken up and appears in a different order as chapters xxvi-xxxi in the Greek; and xxv.15 to the end of the chapter in the Hebrew follows on directly in the Greek as ch.xxxii, after including what corresponds in the Hebrew to xlviii.44. Thus in the Greek version chapter xxv of the Hebrew is directly associated with xlvi-li, forming together chapters xxvi-xxxii of the Greek text. We thus obtain a set of prophecies against the nations listed in xxv. This is a much better arrangement, and demonstrates the unity of the material. The whole section has long been held by scholarly opinion to have been written in substance about the second century B.C.

Leaving aside the obvious Egypt and Babylon, the list of nations denounced is highly significant in this respect. It is virtually the same list as the confederacy in the Biblical Asaph psalm lxxxiii, the peoples against whom Judas Maccabaeus fought (*I.Macc.*v), and the host of the Sons of Darkness with whom the Sons of Light contended according to one of the documents among the Dead Sea Scrolls. It is most unlikely that the similarity is merely a coincidence, and it would seem to point to some community of origins and to a relationship with events of a specific period.

There is clearly established an association between *Jeremiah*, the psalms attributed to Asaph in the Bible, and the Essene literature. It should not therefore come as a surprise that the *Atbash* cipher should be found in the text of *Jeremiah*, evidently by design. When could this have happened? As suggested, it may well have been prior to the translation of the Biblical Prophetic Collection into Greek. But we also have to consider that the text of *Jeremiah* in the Greek reflects a more accurate arrangement of the prophet's pronouncements than the present massoretic Hebrew text in which the cipher occurs.

Some light on the circumstances may be thrown by the fact that there was much destruction and dislocation of the Hebrew sacred books in the period of persecution initiated in the second century B.C. by Antiochus Epiphanes. Interestingly, in the Introductions to *II Maccabees* (ii.13-15) we read how Nehemiah after the return from the Babylonian Exile gathered together the Jewish sacred books into a library. The author then continues: "And in like manner Judas (i.e. Maccabaeus) also gathered together for us all those writings that had been scattered by reason of the war that befell, and they are still with us. If therefore ye (i.e. the Jews of Egypt) have need thereof, send some to fetch them unto you." Both Nehemiah and Judas, who was a priest and chasid, here act in an *Asaph* capacity, as Collector, which is what the Hebrew word signifies.

To reconstitute the sacred library in the middle of the second century B.C. must have called for much work of restoration by the scribes and pious priests, including arrangement of the material, and editorial and other additions. It was such Chasidim who would, for homiletical or expository purposes, introduce the *Atbash* cipher. And we learn from the Chasidic *Book of Jubilees* of the tradition that Jacob bequeathed all his books and the books of his fathers to his son Levi, "That he might preserve them and *renew them* (my italics) for his children until this day" (i.e. circa 130 B.C.).[8]

The Essenes, as we know from the Qumran finds, continued the task of training scribes to make copies of the Biblical books and commentaries on them, as well as much other extra-canonical literature. Even some of their desks and inkwells have been recovered.

## Chapter Twelve

# The Emigrations

With the forerunners of the Essenes their effective corporate history began when they abandoned their own country in order to preserve their faith in purity at a time of great persecution. Their zeal, under guidance, was also to perform an atoning work for the transgressions of many in Israel, so that God might again look upon His people with favour. The Prophet Jeremiah had spoken of a New Covenant, and as we may judge there was one man now who was prepared to draw up its terms, the man we know as the Teacher of Righteousness, or True Teacher.

At this stage of our researches we need further to clarify the beginnings and development of Essene history, in so far as sources of information are now accessible to us. This is essential in order to have a more accurate comprehension of primitive Christianity, both as regards beliefs and circumstances. We have already thrown light on some aspects which were the outcome of Essene doctrine. But now we need to have a clearer image of developments as a foundation for the explorations which will take us so much further afield in time and distance.

In the literature largely represented by the Dead Sea Scrolls there is not a large amount of straightforward information about events and circumstances in the Essene story, due to their deliberate mysteriousness and expository methods. But there is enough, when we have grasped certain of their techniques and can relate what we read about to other sources of information.

We have, I hope, sufficiently clarified that early in the second century B.C. the Jewish people were caught up in a Hellenizing process, which was corrupting the chief priests, and seemed likely to bring about the extinction of Judaism.' The situation became aggravated by the policies of the Syrian ruler of the country, Antiochus Epiphanes.

In these circumstances a body of 'penitents' migrated to the Land of Damascus, the region known as the Hauran. The intention seems to have been that they would remain in exile during the period of apostasy when Belial was let loose against Israel. What we cannot be sure of is whether the True Teacher was with the original body of emigrants, or with others joined them a little later. Certainly, however, he became their leader, and the formulator of the terms of the New Covenant, to which they were required to pledge their allegiance.

Our principal source of information here is the *Damascus Document*. There we read:

And during the period of the destruction of the land there arose those who removed the landmark and led Israel astray. And the land became desolate because they spake rebellion against the commandments of God through Moses . . . and they prophesied a lie to turn away Israel from God.

But God remembered the covenant with the forefathers:
　　And He raised up from Aaron[1] men of understanding,
　　And from Israel wise men:
　　And He made them to hearken,
　　And they digged the well.
　　'A well the princes digged,
　　The nobles of the people delved it
　　By the order of the Lawgiver' (*Num*. xxi. 18).

'The well' is the Law, and 'they who digged it' are the Penitents of Israel who went forth out of the land of Judah and sojourned in the land of Damascus, all of whom God called princes, for they sought Him with a pure heart and His glory was not turned back in the mouth of one of them. And 'the Lawgiver' is the Student of the Law, in regard to whom Isaiah said, 'He bringeth forth an instrument for His work.' And 'the nobles of the people' are those who came to dig the well by the precepts in which the Lawgiver ordained that they should walk throughout the full period of the wickedness."[2]

The Essene interpretation of *Numbers* in the Mosaic books is typical of their methods of exegesis. The significant thing is that by this interpretation the Lawgiver is not Moses, but his ultimate spiritual successor as predicted in *Deuteronomy* xviii. 15. Josephus referred to this when he wrote of the Essenes: "After God they hold most in awe the name of their Lawgiver, any blasphemer of whom is punished with death."[3] This is why the real name of the True Teacher is never given in the Essene documents, only pseudonymous allusions to his status and qualities.

We find the same methods of interpretation in another passage of the same work, which also relates to the emigration.

When the two houses of Israel separated . . . all who proved faithless were delivered to the sword, and those who held fast escaped into the land of the North. As He said, 'And I will cause to go into captivity Siccuth your

king and Chiun your images, the star of your god which ye made for
yourselves, beyond Damascus' (*Amos* v.26-27). The Books of the Law are
the 'tabernacle of the king,' as He said, 'And I will raise up the tabernacle of
David that is fallen' (*Amos* ix.11-12).[4] 'The king' is the Congregation, and
'Chiun the images' are the Books of the Prophets, whose words Israel has
despised. And 'the star' is he who studied the Law, who came to Damascus, as
it is written, 'There shall come forth a star out of Jacob, and a sceptre shall rise
out of Israel' (*Num*.xxiv.17).[5] 'The sceptre' is the prince of the congregation.[6]

In their place of exile, and under the inspiration of the True
Teacher, the emigrants entered into a New Covenant faithfully to
observe the commandments of God according to their true interpretation; and it is evident from our source that they intended to remain
in exile, living a spartan life in camps, until the eve of the anticipated
Messianic deliverance. This proved to be a protracted period, as the
texts disclose, and it becomes all the more important therefore to
determine, if we can, when the True Teacher and his associates left
Judaea. The *Damascus Document* itself comes to our aid in this matter,
in giving the reason for the emigration as the state of apostasy in
Israel in the time of the Seleucid kings.

At the close of a poetic passage of the *Damascus Document* we read:

> And they cast off restraint with a high hand
> To walk in the way of the wicked, of whom God said:
> Their wine is the poison of dragons
> And the cruel venom of asps (*Deut*.xxxii.33).'

'The dragons' are the kings of the Gentiles, and 'the wine' is their ways, and
the 'venom of asps' is the head of the kings of Javan (i.e. the Greek Seleucid
rulers) who came to execute vengeance on them.[7]

A little later we have another allusion to the emigration. The
Penitents "that went forth from the Holy City trusted in God
throughout the period that Israel trespassed and polluted the Sanctuary, and returned again to molten images."[8]

What we have now adduced fully supports what we considered in
chapters two and three. The period of Israel's apostasy was notably
under the Seleucid monarchs Antiochus Epiphanes, Antiochus
Eupator, and Demetrius Soter, roughly between 173 and 153 B.C. It
was particularly under the last of these that the 'Wicked Priest'
Alcimus was active, and the evidence would appear to point very
positively to him as the persecutor of the True Teacher, who sought
to bring about his death. It was Alcimus who particularly attacked
the Chasidim, and this was in the reign of Demetrius.[9] We are
further directed to this reign by a fragment which has survived of the

Essene *Commentary on Nahum*.[10] After citing *Nah*.ii.11, "Where the lion, even the old lion, stalked, there too the cub, and none made them afraid," the interpretation given is, "This is to be explained of Demetrius, king of Javan, who sought to enter Jerusalem on the advice of those who practise flatteries... and none made afraid the kings of Javan from the time of Antiochus down to the rise of the rulers of the Kittim (i.e. the Romans)."

The indications are that the emigration could have taken place around 161-160 B.C. so far as the True Teacher was concerned. There may be an indirect reference in Josephus. Treating of this period he writes:

By what means the nation of the Jews recovered their freedom when they had been brought into slavery by the Macedonians, and what struggles, and how many great battles, Judas, the general of their army, ran through till he was slain as he was fighting for them, has been related in the foregoing book. But after he was dead, all the wicked, and those that transgressed the laws of their fathers, *sprang up again in Judaea*, and grew upon them, and distressed them on every side. A famine also assisted their wickedness, and afflicted their country, *till not a few, who by reason of their want of necessaries, and because they were not able to bear up against their miseries that both the famine and their enemies brought upon them, deserted their country, and went to the Macedonians.* And now Bacchides gathered those Jews together who had apostasised from the accustomed way of living of their forefathers, and chose to live like their neighbours, and committed the care of the country to them; who also caught the friends of Judas, and those of his party, and delivered them up to Bacchides, who, when he had in the first place tortured and tormented them at his pleasure, he by this means at length killed them. And when this calamity of the Jews was become so great, as they had never experienced the like since their return out of Babylon, those that remained of the companions of Judas... came to his brother Jonathan.[11]

This statement from Josephus would seem to be based at least in part on *I.Macc*.ix.23-31, but the second passage I have italicised is not from this source. Josephus was familiar with the Essenes, and had intended joining them, and we can see from his references that he had a fair amount of knowledge about them. He is here alluding to the second persecution of the Jewish religion conducted by Bacchides and the apostate high priest Alcimus around B.C.160.

The *Damascus Document* makes reference not only to the emigrations, but also to the elapse of time which permitted many to fall away from their commitment to the code of the New Covenant. We quote again from this work with its Essene manner of exegesis.

They who hold fast to him are for the life of eternity.
And all the glory of man is for them;

As God confirmed it to them by Ezekiel the prophet, saying:
'The Priests and the Levites and the Sons of Zadok, that kept the charge of
My Sanctuary when the children of Israel went astray from Me,
They shall bring near unto Me fat and blood.'
'The Priests' are the Penitents of Israel who went forth out of the land of
Judah;
And 'the Levites' are they who joined them.
And 'the Sons of Zadok' are the Elect of Israel called by name,
That arise in the End of the Days.
Behold the statement of their names according to their generations,
And the period of their activity, and the number of their afflictions,
And the years of their sojournings and the statement of their works.

Here the categories are not of those who conducted the worship of
the Temple, the natural meaning of the Ezekiel quotation, but of
those who participated in the redemptive activity by adherence to
the New Covenant. The pioneer emigrants were the Penitents of
Israel, and these were followed over a period of uncertain duration
by others who fled from Judaea to join their ranks. Of this second
phase we hear again in the so-called *Psalms of Solomon*:

And Jerusalem did all things according as the Gentiles did in their cities to
their gods . . . and there was none amongst them that did mercy and truth in
Jerusalem. They that loved the assemblies of the Saints fled away from them;
and they flew like sparrows who fly from their nests. And they were
wandering in the wilderness, in order to save their souls from evil; and
precious was the sojourning with them of any soul that was saved from them
(i.e. the wicked).[13]

The rules of the New Covenanters were strict, and the conditions
of life in their camps in inhospitable regions were severe. Many fell
away finding the Essene discipline too strenuous for them. Some
were expelled for breaches of the regulations. Some gave up and left
of their own accord. We are told in the *Damascus Document* that God
hates and abhors the apostates, and continues: "So are all the men
who entered into the New Covenant in the land of Damascus, and
yet turned backward and acted treacherously and departed from the
spring of living waters."[14] And again: "With a judgement like unto
that of their neighbours, who turned aside with the scornful men,
shall they be judged. For they spake error against the statutes of
righteousness, and rejected the Covenant and the pledge of faith,
which they affirmed in the land of Damascus; and this is the New
Covenant."[15] Since the recovery of so many of the Essene documents
we have become aware that as a sect the Essenes were very harsh and
puritanical, and hardly at all a kindly, benevolent, spiritual body of

people as they are often represented in fiction.

The voluntary exile of the New Covenanters was not designed to be permanent. They looked forward to a redemptive climax to their sufferings when the period of the Wickedness should be ended; and the indications are that in the reign of Herod the Great in Judaea a substantial number of them returned to the region of the Dead Sea to await the coming of the Great Deliverance. The Qumran settlement developed accordingly, representing the third, or *Sons of Zadok* period, that of the Elect of Israel at the End of the Days.

### Chapter Thirteen

# Pentecost

From references to the Essenes in Josephus and Philo, and from some passages in ancient Church writers, notably Eusebius and Epiphanius in the fourth century A.D., it had long been possible to know that there had been a close relationship, if not an actual identity, between the Essenes and the Nazoreans (Judaeo-Christians). But since the modern dramatic discovery of the Dead Sea Scrolls we have positive evidence, unwelcome to committed Christians because of its implications, that the relationship had been more circumstantial than could be confirmed previously. Much that was set down in the New Testament had now to be looked at quite differently, not as something novel in concepts and language, but as an unacknowledged and largely unrecognised indebtedness to initial close Essene associations.

From the activities of John the Baptist and of Jesus until at least the destruction of Jerusalem by the Romans in 70 A.D. the homeland of Christianity was Galilee and Judaea, and its principal adherents were Jews, who did not by their conviction of the Messiahship of Jesus change their religion. And even with the Apostle Paul, his conversion and immediately subsequent experiences arose from contacts which were Jewish; and since the find of the Dead Sea Scrolls he can be seen more clearly to have been under Essene influences.

But the Essene connection, of no interest or concern as such to the Graeco-Roman world, is not declared, though it is covered by references to the Saints, the Poor, and those of the Way. Only Jewish bodies which were somewhat different, such as the Pharisees, or positively antagonistic, such as the Sadducees, are referred to directly by name.

We have to ask whether, without the prior existence and propaganda of the Essenes, their Messianic beliefs, their organization and discipline, Christianity would have come into existence at all. Would even Jesus himself have become convinced that he was the Teacher and Messiah of the End Time if the Essenes had not determined the period in their anticipations? What has to come to us is the overwhelming realisation that the commencement of our era was unique in history in that of no other time previously was it postulated that the climax of the Ages had been reached. Awareness of this must be with us continually with every word we read of the Dead Sea Scrolls, the Apocalyptic literature, and the New Testament. Today we are looking backward over nearly twenty centuries which have elapsed since the advent of the End Time was believed to have come, and consequently our consciousness and interpretations have been dulled and confused by that fact. We need to school our imagination to the imminence of the consummation, by contemplating it in terms such as these:

And the angel which I saw stand upon the sea and upon the earth lifted up his hand to heaven, and sware by Him that liveth for ever and ever, who created heaven, and the things that therein are, and the earth, and the things that therein are, and the sea, and the things which are therein, that there should be Time no longer: but in the days of the voice of the seventh angel, when he shall begin to sound his trumpet, the Mystery of God should be finished, as He hath declared to his servants the prophets (*Rev.*x.5-7).

Thus what happened in Palestine in the first century of our era was conditioned by a sense of haste. A protracted period of development for the Messianic Community was not anticipated. The Community had been formed at Jerusalem at the festival of Pentecost. The *Acts of the Apostles* reports the event in dramatic terms; but it does not offer any explanation of why it should have happened at Pentecost, or how it came about that a handful of Galilean peasants and fishermen could create almost overnight a quite elaborate form of communal government suited to a sudden influx of many thousands of Jewish adherents from many lands. Whence came the practice of communal meetings on the first day of the week, and the appointment of officials, a trio at the head, and area Supervisors (Bishops) and Administrators (Deacons)?

The answer is that everything was ready to hand in the Essene organization and practices. From our sources we learn that Pentecost was the chief Essene festival, and we discover how the manner in which it was celebrated affected what we think of as the Early Church. One of our oldest sources is the *Book of Jubilees*, dating from around the middle of the second century B.C., a work highly venerated by the Essenes. It professes indeed to be in accordance with the Law and Commandments delivered to Moses on Sinai.

The book employs a solar calendar, and not a solar-lunar one, dividing time into a series of Jubilees on the basis of the number 7, each year consisting of 52 weeks of seven days, and each jubilee representing seven times seven years. The length of the year would be 364 days. Since the Creation of the world had begun on the first day of the first week of the first year – that is on a Sunday – it followed that Nisan 1, the commencement of the first month of the Jewish year, must always fall on a Sunday. And what was more, in this system, *Shevuot*, the Jewish Feast of Weeks (Pentecost), would also always be on a Sunday, corresponding to the fifteenth day of the third month, Sivan.

Thus the Essene Pentecost did not exactly correspond to that of the Pharisees, and was invariably celebrated on a Sunday. It was regarded as the chief festival, as Philo notes with regard to the Therapeuts of Egypt.[1] It was held to commemorate God's covenant with Noah after the Flood. Prior to the Flood the Feast of Weeks had been celebrated in Heaven from the first day of Creation; but now it began to be celebrated on earth as a sign of God's covenant with Man.

In the terms of that covenant, as we read in *Genesis ix*.4, the eating of flesh with the blood in it was expressly forbidden. This should be noted, because it is said in the *Acts of the Apostles* (xv.20) that when the Apostle Paul sought permission for converted Gentiles to be admitted to the Christian Community it was made a condition that they must observe the Primeval Laws (Laws of Noah), including refraining from eating blood. There is some reason for thinking that this ruling was given at a convocation held in Jerusalem at Pentecost.

The Pharisees identified Pentecost as the day of the Giving of the Law on Sinai. But for the Essenes the festival also signified the renewal of the Law, by entering into the New Covenant drawn up by the True Teacher. Their influence on the followers of Jesus is suggested by the remark in the *Acts of the Apostles* (vi.7) that "the number of the disciples multiplied in Jerusalem greatly; and *a great number of the priests were obedient to the faith.*"

With the Essenes, many of whom were priests, the festival of Pentecost had given rise to an annual convocation at this season which, as they said, was to continue "for as long as the dominion of Satan endures."[2] Because Pentecost was the festival of Renewal of the Covenant it was made a time of assembly for representatives of all Essene communities, who pledged again their loyalty to their New Covenant. Their status was reassessed, disputes and misconduct were dealt with, and on the same occasion new applicants for membership took their oath of allegiance to observe the Covenant of the Law.

One of the translators of the Scrolls, Dr. Vermes, has written about the occasion as follows:

The most important of their festivals was the Feast of Weeks, the Feast of the Renewal of the Covenant. Its ritual is described at the beginning of the *Community Rule* and in an unpublished section of the *Damascus Rule*. Opening the ceremony, the Priests and Levites offer blessings to God and those entering the Covenant with them reply, 'Amen, Amen. The Priests go on to recall the past favours of God, and the Levites follow them with a recital of Israel's transgressions. This culminates in a public confession, 'We have strayed! We have disobeyed!' etc., after which the penitents are blessed by the Priests. Then the Levites pronounce a long curse on the 'lot of Satan', and with the Priests they solemnly adjure all those whose repentance is incomplete not to enter the Covenant. 'Cursed be the man', they say, 'who enters this Covenant while walking among the idols of his heart . . . He shall be cut off from the midst of the Sons of Light and . . . his lot shall be among them that are cursed for ever'.

The Pentecost ritual plainly looks back to the account in *Deuteronomy* of the blessings and curses of the Covenant recited to the people of Israel on Mounts Gerizim and Ebal (*Deut.*xxvii).

Turning to the Pentecost story in the *Acts of the Apostles* we have the speech of Peter calling the people to repentance, urging them to "Save yourselves from this untoward generation" (ii.38-40). As with the Essenes those who join the Community hand over all their possessions or the value of them. And we are told of the case of Ananias and his wife Sapphira, who kept back part of the price received for their property. Clearly they had entered into the Covenant "while walking among the idols of their hearts". They were of "the lot of Satan", and so we read that they were struck dead, "and great fear came upon all who heard these things."[4]

To any who may question the connection between the first Christian Community and the Essenes, we have the further confirmation of the speech of Stephen the proto-martyr given in the *Acts* which contains passages based on the Essene *Assumption of Moses*, one of them being a direct quotation.

Reverting here to the theme of organization, Pentecost was the occasion when the Essenes held their chief convocation. It was then that matters of dispute or misdemeanour could be settled by the chief officers and court, if it had been necessary to have them referred here by local communities. The practice was evidently incorporated into the Christian organization. Their central authority met in Jerusalem under the Presidency of Jacob (James), the brother of Jesus.[5] Associated with him were Peter and John, thus forming the Trio corresponding to that of the Essenes, and called by Paul "the pillars" (*Gal*.ii.9). One of the important matters this body had to consider was the terms of admission of Believing Gentiles into the Messianic Community, and we may infer that the ruling was given at a Pentecost Convocation. For this there is some supporting evidence.

Paul, as we learn from his Epistles, opposed the view that Gentile converts should be required to become full Jews and observe the Jewish holy days. Many have concluded that Paul himself had ceased to be an observant Jew. Yet in the *Acts of the Apostles* we find him abandoning his missionary work in distant lands more than once at a most promising juncture, and making the long and arduous journey to Jerusalem for the express purpose of keeping a Jewish festival.

This happened once at Ephesus in Asia Minor, where the Jews there had begged him to stay and instruct them. But Paul replied, "I must by all means keep this feast that cometh in Jerusalem: but I will return again unto you, if God will" (*Acts* xviii.21). In another year we find Paul sailing past Ephesus, and not landing there, for, as the author says, "he hasted, if it were possible for him, to be at Jerusalem the day of Pentecost" (*Acts* xx.16).

The references, I think, point to an imperative for Paul to get to Jerusalem from wherever he was, if at all practicable, at the season of Pentecost. And this was because he was required to make his report on his activities (*Acts* xxi.18-19). Pentecost would then have been employed by the Christians in the same way as the Essenes, as an annual occasion for taking stock on matters of consequence coming up for decisions at the highest level. If this is correct it substantially changes Christian understanding of the relationship between the Apostle Paul and the Jerusalem leaders, and between the communities he established among the Gentiles and the supreme Judaeo-Christian Council.[6] We can even see that, when the ruling was made regarding the Gentile converts, Jacob in his address (*Acts* xv.13-18) employs the Essene manner of exegesis.

For Paul the authority of the Council at Jerusalem was paramount, as the Government of all who gave their allegiance to Jesus as Messiah. It had been officially constituted as the outcome of the manifestation of the Spirit at Pentecost, and his converts had no standing in Israel without its endorsement.

Consistent with this is a fragment of manuscript found among the Dead Sea Scrolls, and believed to be part of the Essene liturgy for Pentecost. We read: "But in the time of Thy goodwill Thou didst choose for Thyself a people. Thou didst remember Thy Covenant and didst grant that they should be set apart for Thyself from among all the peoples as a holy thing. And Thou didst renew for them Thy Covenant, founded on a glorious vision and the words of Thy Holy Spirit."

*Chapter Fourteen*

# Those of the Way

We are now in process of acquiring an understanding of the beginnings of Christianity which was not previously practicable. There is even in the New Testament a great deal that has not been rightly understood and allusions which are not developed or explained.

A case in point is the reference to 'the Way' in the *Acts of the Apostles* (ix.2,xxii.4). The term is used by Paul as an apparently current description, familiar to many, of the particular Jewish sectarians to whom formerly he had been violently hostile. What did the expression signify, and did it relate peculiarly to the followers of Jesus? The answer comes to us very clearly. 'The Way' is primarily God's way of salvation, the Way of the Lord, prepared before Him by His messenger, and cutting a path through the wilderness, as predicted by the Prophets.[1] But it assumed under the Essenes a more particular connotation. As a consequence, 'those of the Way' are not simply the Christians, but all those who sought in an apostate time to advance the cause of the Kingdom of God. Of necessity, therefore, for the Penitents of Israel the Way of the Lord was the Way of His Law, which they covenanted to keep. It was to follow this way that they had emigrated to the Land of Damascus.[2] Their *Community Rule* instructed the faithful:

They shall separate from the habitation of ungodly men, and shall go into the wilderness to prepare the Way of Him; as it is written, 'Prepare ye in the wilderness the Way of the Lord . . .' This (Way) is the study of the Law which He commanded by the hand of Moses, that they may do according to all that has been revealed by His holy Spirit" (VIII).

Only by faithfulness to the Way would Israel obtain deliverance, and this was the message of John the Baptist, the Messianic personality who appeared from the wilderness.

The Christian interpretation of the Baptist's function is familiar to us from the opening words of the *Gospel of Mark*, and also in *Luke* (i.76-77) from the words of the priest Zechariah about his son John: "And thou, child, shalt be called the prophet of the Highest: for thou shalt go before the face of the Lord to prepare His ways; to give knowledge of salvation unto His people for the remission of their sins."

The scene of the Baptist's activities was not far from the Essene settlements in the vicinity of the Dead Sea, and it has long been held that there was a link between his followers and the Essenes, and also between the Baptists and the Zealots who had followed Judas of Galilee at the beginning of the first century A.D. The link is clearly conveyed in the Old Russian version of Josephus's *Jewish War*. There it is said of John: "He came to the Jews and summoned them to freedom, saying, 'God hath sent me to show you the Way of the Law, whereby you may free yourselves from many masters; and there shall be no mortal ruling over you, but only the Highest who has sent me.'"[3] The slogan of the followers of Judas of Galilee was "No ruler but God."

In the references to Paul's attack on the followers of 'the Way' there is no explanation of why, with the authority of the Sadducean high priest he should have taken the road to Damascus to make his arrests. Why should he specifically go to that remote area, when we are told (*Acts* viii. 1) that those he was seeking "were all scattered abroad throughout the region of Judaea and Samaria"? The movement associated with Jesus was far too new at this time to have a substantial branch in the Damascus region. And what of the mysterious Ananias of Damascus whom Paul was to encounter in this city, and who spoke to him of the "Just One"?[4]

Everything becomes much more intelligible when we appreciate that the followers of the True Teacher as the Just One, or rather their precursors, had – as we have related – removed to the Damascus region, where by Paul's time their communities had existed for nearly two hundred years. The area in which they were to be found had become a place of refuge and activity for sectarians, dissidents, freedom fighters and outlaws. We learn something of this from the pages of Josephus and from Rabbinical sources. One of the Essene terms for the region was 'the wilderness of the peoples.' The peoples included the vestigial remnants of various races from the remote past.

Turning to Josephus we find that he records that about B.C. 23 Augustus Caesar had transferred to the jurisdiction of Herod the Great the countries of Trachonitis, Batanea and Auranitis (Bashan and the Hauran). The reason given was the behaviour of a certain

Zenodorus, who "was perpetually setting the brigands of Trachonitis to molest the inhabitants of Damascus."[5] Herod, therefore, having acquired the territory, sought to make it safe from marauders who preyed upon the Jewish pilgrims from the East. Here we quote Josephus again.

When Herod learned that a Jew from Babylonia had crossed the Euphrates with five hundred horsemen, all of them mounted archers, and a group of kinsmen amounting to a hundred men . . . he sent for this man and his band of followers, promising to give them land in the toparchy called Batanea, which bordered on Trachonitis, for he wished to make a buffer zone out of such a settlement, and he promised that this land should be free of taxes and that they should be exempt from all the customary forms of tribute, for he would permit them to settle on the land without obligation.

Being persuaded by this offer, the Babylonian went there to take possession of the land and build on it fortresses and a village, to which he gave the name of Bathyra. This man was a shield both to the inhabitants exposed to the Trachonites and to the Jews who came from Babylonia to sacrifice in Jerusalem; these he kept from being harmed by the brigandage of the Trachonites. And there came to him many men – and from all parts – who were *devoted to the ancestral customs of the Jews*."[6]

The turbulent territory appears to have been linked to what Pliny significantly calls the Nazerine tetrarchy, a name still preserved by that mysterious people the Nusairiyeh, as we shall see.

But to follow Josephus further. He had some knowledge of the area we are considering, since he was the Jewish commander in the North at the beginning of the Jewish war with the Romans in 66 A.D. He later surrendered to the enemy and went over to their side, and in his subsequent accounts exhibited a bitter hostility towards the patriots and messianists who were the backbone of the revolt, especially those in his own command, whom he disparagingly describes as "a mob from Trachonitis, Gaulanitis, Hippos and Gadara, seditionists and fugitives, to whom their infamous careers in peace-time gave war its attractions."[8]

The Pharisees, founders of Rabbinical Judaism were, for their own reasons, antagonistic to the Jewish sectaries, the *minim*. One reason was the tragic consequences of Zealot militancy in the struggles with the Romans. The Rabbis of the first and second centuries after Christ had plenty of opportunity to become acquainted with the sectaries, especially when the seat of rabbinical authority was transferred to Tiberias in Galilee. They were strongly opposed to the Judaeo-Christians (the *Notzrim*, otherwise Nazoreans), but not much less to the Essenes, especially after the disastrous Second Revolt against the Romans under Bar-Cochbar in 133 A.D. inspired by messianic faith. The teaching of the Essenes was held to be heretical, but especially denounced were the *giljonim*, the revelations and apocalyptic literature of the Jewish sectaries,[9] because these encouraged resistance to Rome and expectations of Divine intervention to usher in the Messianic Age. The early Christians were devotees of the apocalyptic books of the Essenes, and themselves produced the *Revelation* in the New Testament which predicted the imminent doom of Rome. The Hebrew word for Apocalypse led to rabbinical puns on the Greek word for Gospel (*Evangelion*) such as *Aven-giljon* (idolatrous revelation) and *Avon-giljon* (iniquitous revelation).[10]

As typifying the Jewish sectaries the rabbis seized on the person of Gehazi, the servant of the Prophet Elisha in the Bible. They asked, "Why did Elisha go to Damascus?" It was to call Gehazi to repentance. But Gehazi replies, "Thus have I received from thee, that whoever has sinned, and has caused the multitude to sin, is given no chance of repentance."[11]

The natural course for those of the Way escaping the persecution instigated by Saul of Tarsus was to seek refuge in the region of the Hauran, especially as there had long been communities of the Saints there to give them asylum.[12] Many of the new refugees were followers of Jesus, and we have a tradition about this persecution preserved in the *Clementine Recognitions* (I.lxxi). There it is reported that some 5,000 of the disciples made for Jericho, the area where were the Essene settlements near the Dead Sea. There they learnt that Saul was hastening to Damascus because he believed that Peter had fled there.

Another tradition comes to us from the Mandaeans, who actually call themselves Nazoreans. The sect originally deriving from the Baptists, still survives in the marsh lands of the Lower Euphrates. One of their texts, discussed by Dr Rudolf Macuch,[13] relates to a persecution at Jerusalem that can be dated in 37 A.D. Matthew Black comments, "It is possible that we have to do with a movement of Christians, emigrating from Palestine'" and this would tie in with the persecution of Saul. The claim of the Mandaean *Haran Gawaita* is that these Nazoreans fled from Judaea and found asylum in the Hauran. The number given is 60,000, but we should probably read 6,000, a figure more comparable to that given in the *Clementine*

*Recognitions.* "A line in the baptismal hymns," writes Lady Drower, "'with Hauran our garment, in Hauraran our cover' may hint that these place-names refer to geographical districts and that they once afforded concealment and cover to refugees for religion's sake."[14]

The Damascus region and the Hauran were the areas from which later the *Book of Shem*[15] was to emanate, and we now have many evidences that here, in spite of many changes and vicissitudes, the Essene-Nazorean teachings and traditions were carried on from century to century.

*Chapter Fifteen*

# The Melting Pot

We have now clarified by a number of evidences that the region to the north-east of Palestine had afforded asylum to a succession of Jewish refugees and sectaries fleeing from persecution and seeking to practice their faith according to their convictions. As time passed there was much mingling of these groups and interchanges of literature and ideas. There was also in the circumstances a tendency of some to become more eccentric and exotic, and for fresh groups to be formed as the course of time threw up new teachers and prophets. Then in the fourth century, when a Christian orthodoxy was established by the Church Councils of the Roman Empire, the former sects were supplemented by the influx of those denounced as heretics. Later still there had to be adjustment to living under the aegis of militant Islam.

We have already made reference to the Nusairijeh,[1] who have continued down to the present day, like the Druses. The Islamic references illustrate that, like the Mandaean-Nazoreans, the Nusairiyeh had absorbed ideas from various sources in the course of their history. Their existence, as well as their name, remains, however, a link with the past which may not be ignored.

These people take us back to those pre-Christian Nasarenes or Nosarenes described by Epiphanius in the fourth century A.D. as surviving in Gilead and Bashan. By religion, according to the Church Father, these Nasarenes were a kind of Jews, but more closely related in their beliefs to the Dosithean Samaritans. They held that they were in possession of the true Law of Moses, which differed from that of the Jews, just as did the Samaritans. In this respect, says Epiphanius, they were like the Osseans, by whom we should no doubt understand the Essaeans (Essenes). He may have had some report of the Law as set forth by the True Teacher in the Land of Damascus.

Bishop Epiphanius, when he devoted himself to describing and seeking to trace the connections of a variety of sects in his monumental

*Panarion*, managed to pick up a great deal of important information. But he slipped up in analysing it and in dealing with nomenclatures. Not only did he have problems with Essenes and Ossenes, Essaeans and Osseans, but also with those he calls Jessaeans. The Christians had for a time been called Jessaeans, he alleges, but he was not sure whether they got this designation from Jesse the father of King David, or from the name Jesus, which – he says – signified in Hebrew the same at the Greek *Therapeutes*, namely 'healer' or 'saviour'.[2] Epiphanius could make a distinction between the Nazoreans and the Nazirites, appreciating that the latter were ascetics. The description Nazir came later to be used by Jews for Dervish.

The variety of Jewish and Judaeo-Christian sects flourishing in the Middle-East was evidently very extensive and considerably inter-related. We meet not only with the familiar Pharisees, Sadducees, Essenes and Nazoreans, but with Elchesaites, Sampseans, Ebionites, Hemerobaptists, Dositheans, etc., etc. The attempt to catalogue and describe them developed, as we have pointed out, as a direct conse-quence of the establishment of a more rigid Christian orthodoxy.

The concern of the Church was especially with Jewish sectaries, who were seen as much more of a danger to its tenets. Converts from Judaism were accordingly carefully screened, and compelled to disavow any possible former associations or sympathies.

We may cite part of a profession of faith of Eastern origin required of converts from Judaism, which is attached to the *Clementine Recognitions*. "I anathematise the Nazareans, the stubborn ones, who deny that the law of sacrifices was given by Moses, who abstain from eating living things, and who never offer sacrifice. I anathematise the Osseans, the blindest of all men, who use other Scriptures than the Law . . ."[3]

The Church Councils were very uncomfortable about the Essenes and were down also on any one with even the faintest hint of Judaising. Nestorius in the fifth century was regarded as a particular offender. Dr Parkes writes:

In the controversy between Nestorians and Chalcedonians, the Nestorians are constantly called 'Jews'. The synod of Ephesus writes to Nestorius, and heads its letter: 'The Holy Synod to Nestorius the new Jew.' The emperor Anastasius, in opening a council to discuss the theology of Macedonius the Nestorian patriarch of Constantinople some seventy years later, begins his address with the words: 'Have you not seen what this Jew who is amongst us did?' Two hundred years later, at the Council *in Trullo*, a reference is made to those who follow the doctrine of Nestorius, separating the natures of Christ, and 'reviving Jewish impiety'.[4]

In the ancient Jewish Gospel parody, the *Toldoth Jeshu*, Nestorius figures as a teacher who instructed the followers of Jesus to adhere faithfully to the Mosaic Law as Jesus himself had done.[5] That the Nestorians were in contact with the Judaeo-Christians, or at least in possession of some of their literature is almost certain. The *Gospel of the Hebrews* used by the Nazoreans, and also the Nazorean *Acts of the Apostles*, could be studied by orthodox authorities like Epiphanius and Jerome. Not long ago there was found in the Shehid 'Ali Pasha collection in Istanbul an Arabic manuscript of the tenth century entitled *The Establishment of Proofs of the Prophethood of Our Master Mohammed*.[6] This work contains a number of very valuable reflections of Judaeo-Christian teaching and views in documents dating from around the sixth or seventh century A.D. The author of the work, 'Abd al-Jabbar, seems to have obtained his material from documents preserved in monasteries of Khuzistan which had been rendered from Syriac into Arabic. The monasteries in Iraq in question would appear to have been Nestorian, and the Judaeo-Christians responsible for the texts employed were evidently located in the region of Mosul and also have had to do with Harran.

The persecutions which had brought so many religious refugees to the North-East of Palestine in earlier times were now being repeated. This time, as we have seen, the Orthodox Christians were the persecutors, and a consequence was a new trek of the victims eastward to the territory of the more tolerant Persia of the Sassanian kings. The Mandaean-Nazoreans had gone this way, the reverse of the route anciently followed by Abraham. Now others were journeying from the Hauran to Harran,[7] and beyond. Some would eventually reach Afghanistan.

With the dynamic rise and missionary zeal of Islam a new problem arose for the sectaries. To continue to survive they had largely to make an outward profession of faith and conformity to the tenets of the Muslims. This was not too difficult or repugnant, since there was much that was Jewish in the new religion. There was belief in the Divine Unity, the acceptance of Jesus as wholly human and as a true prophet. Mohammed himself had learnt much from Judaeo-Christian contacts.

Time and circumstances had brought about a progressive change of emphasis. Political Messianism was now largely replaced by a Spiritual Messianism, leaning towards the Essene figure of the True Teacher in the guise' of Jesus as the True Prophet,[8] whose mantle had fallen on the Prophet Mohammed himself.

Harried and persecuted as they were, the sects persisted. Such bodies are very tenacious of existence. But as it happened they were to receive an unexpected stimulus in the ninth century. At its beginning there was a chance discovery in the region of Jericho of a hoard of Hebrew manuscripts of the same order as those we call the Dead Sea Scrolls. This find, larger than the modern one, brought the Essene teachings back into currency with a vengeance. Timotheus, Metropolitan of Seleucia, reporting the find, thought that the manuscripts might have been hidden away by the Prophet Jeremiah. We have already given some information about this discovery.[9]

What happened to the manuscripts we have no means of knowing. But it would seem that copies were made and also translations of some of the texts into various languages. The latter at least circulated widely and effected a substantial revival of interest in lost and forgotten Essene literature and ideas. Particularly influenced were the new Jewish sect of Karaites in the ninth and tenth century, who hailed the documents as the legacy of the Sages of the Second Temple. The Karaites had a considerable community at Constantinople, where they found some favour with the Byzantines as being in opposition to Rabbinical Judaism.

The texts utilised by the Karaites are attributed to the *Magharriyah* (Men of the Caves), because as the Karaite author Kirkisani explains, their books were found in a cave (*maghar*).[10] Among the texts Kirkisani mentions a *Book of Zadok*, a *Book of Yadua*, the works of the Alexandrian (almost certainly Philo), and many strange commentaries on the Scriptures, evidently of the same order as those found at Qumran. In his *Kitab al-Anwar* (*Book of Lights*) he refers to teachings comparable to those in the Essene *Damascus Document*, retrieved in Hebrew manuscripts by S. Schechter from the *geniza* (lumber-room) of the Karaite synagogue in Old Cairo and published in 1910.[11]

We have now traced the Essene story and its Messianic concepts from its Chasidic beginnings in the second century B.C. through the period of Essene impact on Jewish life and thought out of which Christianity emerged. And we have now briefly reported on the strange flowering of its concepts in the tenth century of our era, which was to spread them far and wide. In Part Two we shall seek to trace and follow these subsequent developments down to the present day. But we shall also delve into legends and traditions which convey that someone like the True Teacher finally travelled to the East and ended his days in Kashmir.

Amidst the trials and travails of the sects which inherited elements of the Essene mysteries and eschatology (teachings about the Last Times) recollections of the original True Teacher had tended to disappear. But suddenly, when the hoard of Essene literature was discovered near Jericho at the beginning of the ninth century there was remembrance of him again, and the representative names of Joseph and Asaph, even combined as Joasaph and Yus-asaph, were back in circulation.

# PART TWO

### Chapter One

# The Ghost Goes West

With this second division of our exploration we shall be concerned with the period approximately from the tenth to the twentieth century, and our pursuit of information will take us very far afield. It will also become more difficult, because we shall be unable to rely to any great extent on precise and positive evidences. Indeed, the quest on which we are embarked has never previously been undertaken in the form demanded by what has come before us in Part One. We have keys and clues denied to other investigators. These will call for close attention on the reader's part, but he or she will have the thrill of perceiving connections and associations. I have sought to make these exercises not too strenuous both in the text, and by reference to the notes, and no effort has been spared in assembling rare and remote witnesses. We are involved in a tremendously significant job together, which entitles us to wish ourselves 'good luck and good hunting'.

One of our problems is that we are largely dealing with the exotic East where ways of presenting information are not governed by the rules to which we are more accustomed, and where legend plays a considerable part. The accounts given were more concerned with reporting and entertaining than with being strictly factual. There is also the difficulty with the ancient oriental texts that not only are they in various languages and dialects, but the narration of events uses a variety of systems of chronology.

Our quest will begin with the West. This is because, thanks to the Crusades, and the westward advance of Islam, with many Jews among the Muslims, much material – literature and ideas – was coming into Europe from the Near and Middle East, some of it religious and esoteric. This included the legacies of the Essenes.

In the last chapter of Part One we have seen how the hoard of manuscripts found near Jericho at the beginning of the ninth century had a very strong influence on the Jewish sect of Karaites which was spreading into eastern Europe. It was Karaite missionaries who were in no small measure responsible for the forms of Judaism adopted by the Khazars of South Russia, and who were involved in the Judaizing heresy which spread through Russia in the Middle Ages and persisted for centuries. Centres of its activity were Novgorod and Kiev. In the fifteenth century we learn particularly of the doctrine taught by the Karaite Zechariah of Kiev. Robert Eisler, citing Josif of Volokolamsk, says that:

Zechariah taught his disciples that the belief in a triune God was vain; that there was but one God; that Jesus was not the Son of God nor the Messiah, but only a prophet like Moses, and therefore could not have risen from the dead; and that the Messiah had not yet appeared, but would come at the end of time, and even then not as Son of God *according to his essence*, but only *according to his works*, like Moses and the prophets of old. Consequently, until then the Law of Moses was binding; the Sabbath and the food laws must continue to be observed, and the veneration of icons and saints shunned as idolatrous . . ."

There can be no doubt that a considerable amount of Essene and kindred literature had been coming into circulation in Europe, since we find translations of some of the documents into Armenian, Georgian, Lithuanian, Roumanian, and Slavonic. We also encounter versions of Josephus containing important statements relating to Jesus and John the Baptist.[2] But much doctrine was being spread by word of mouth, sometimes in secret, giving rise to various sects, notably the Bogomils, Cathars and Albigenses.

We may single out for special mention, however, the sect of Josephinists found in Northern Italy and Provence in the thirteenth century. This sect had already been known to the ecclesiastical authorities in the previous century. To quote Eisler again:-

The term (*Josepini, Josephini, Josephistae*) first occurs in a decree of Pope Lucius III and the Council of Verona (1184), in a bull of Gregory IX of 1231, and in charters of the Emperor Frederick II (1239) always in the fixed formula 'circumcisos, passaginos, Josephinos,' from which one may infer that it is a question of Judaists practising circumcision. The term *passaginos*, of doubtful meaning, most probably indicates 'vagabonds', 'vaganti', corresponding to the *strojniki*, the 'straying apostles' of the Bulgarian Bogomils – that is, people who leave their settled homes and take up a wanderer's life from religious convictions.[3]

It has been suggested that this curiously named roving sect was in some way linked with the name of the Jewish historian Josephus. And there is this possibility in the way legends developed, since Josephus had written about the Essenes, while yet there was an inner association with the significant names Joseph and Asaph handed down from the past. We noted, for example, the allusion by Andronicus to "Asaph the writer and *historian* of the Hebrews."[4]

Whatever may be the truth about the Josephists, or Josephistans, we have the important fact around the tenth century – when versions of Essene books can be deemed to have reached the West – that a work from the Middle East was gaining great favour in Europe under the title *Barlaam and Josaphat*. It was a book well thought of by the Cathars, but was popular with the orthodox also, so that it entered into the lives of the saints in the *Golden Legend* of Jacques de Voragine in the thirteenth century. This tale, as we shall show, proves to be of the utmost importance in our quest.

Barlaam and Josaphat (initially Joasaph), the principal personalities in the book, were believed to have been real people and not fictional characters. They were given a festal day in the Christian calendars of the Greek, Russian and Roman Churches. A church at Palermo, Sicily, was dedicated to 'Divo Josaphat', and even relics believed to be of his body were presented in 1571 to King Sebastian of Portugal by the Doge of Venice, Luigi Mocenigo. These included part of his spine. They eventually found their way to Antwerp.

A great deal of mystery surrounds the origin of the book. It has been held to have been a product of eastern Manichaeism; but what is certain is that the narrative has largely borrowed from the life of Gautama the Buddha, and the Josaphat (Joasaph) of the story is the Buddha's counterpart. This was already appreciated by Diego do Couto, a Portuguese writer, in the seventeenth century.

Joasaph is the goodly child of an Indian monarch noted for his excesses. Told by an astrologer that the infant would eventually embrace Christianity, the king segregates his son in a special palace and surrounds him with every luxury and delight, so that he shall not encounter the world's miseries. Growing up, he became weary of his restricted existence, and reluctantly the king permitted him to leave his compound. There in the real world he discovered the existence of disease and death, and was filled with sorrow and despair. In these circumstances he was visited by the monk Barlaam in the guise of a merchant. A friendship developed between the two, and eventually Joasaph not only became a Christian, but he also abandoned his royal state and became *a wandering ascetic* (my italics).

This is an all too brief description of the essence of the narrative;

but it illustrates the similarities of the plot to the familiar features of the early life of the Buddha.

The sub-title of the Greek version of *Barlaam and Joasaph* describes the books as: "An edifying story from the inner land of the Ethiopians, called the land of the Indians, thence brought to the Holy City, by John the Monk (an honourable man and virtuous, of the monastery of Saint Sabas); wherein are the lives of the famous and blessed Barlaam and Joasaph." John the monk is here credited with having brought the manuscript to Jerusalem from the monastery of Mar Saba between Jerusalem and Jericho.

It has been suggested that it may have been because of this allusion to John the Monk that the book was credited to St. John of Damascus, who had contact with Eastern thought and literature, and who flourished in the eighth century. The Greek version, however, did not appear until some three hundred years later, derived – it is claimed – from an earlier Georgian text, and the first to Christianise the Buddha story. In the Georgian version *Barlaam* appears as *Balahvar* and *Joasaph* as *Jodasaph*. Based on the story, a Georgian hymn existed already in the tenth century in praise of the Blessed Jodasaph.

But where did the Georgian Christians acquire the tale they utilised? There can be no doubt that this was from an Arabic work relating to the Buddha, which was circulating in Iraq in the tenth century, and is referred to in the famous *Kitab al-Fihrist* dating from A.D.987-988. Of three such works mentioned, one was called *Kitab Bilawhar wa-Yudasaf*. In another document by a Muslim author of the same period Yudasaf is listed as a false prophet, and placed in time between Zoroaster and Mani.[5]

The view hitherto taken about the name Yudasaf in the West, because of the association with the Buddha, is that the name reflects the word for a Buddha designate, namely *Bodhisattva*. While this is not impossible, it does not adequately account for the change of Joasaph, and in another context Jusasaph.[6] It also appears significant, following upon the evidences in Part One which we have produced, that this enlistment of a great teacher like the Buddha should have coincided in point of time with the rediscovery of the nameless True Teacher of the Dead Sea Scrolls, with whom were linked the designations Joseph and Asaph. Additionally, around the same period the name of the historian Josephus comes to the fore, termed in the Middle East *Yusiphus*.

There are some elements of mystery here which call for further explorations, even if the results cannot lead us to positive conclusions. And here is another of them. The Introduction to the Greek text of *Barlaam and Joasaph* associates Ethiopia with India, and this association is made by other ancient writers. The *Barlaam and Joasaph* story, especially in the Arabic and Hebrew versions, contains a number of fables, some of which derive from Indian sources, as do the later fables collected under the venerable name of AEsop (i.e. the Ethiopian).[7] The likeness to Asaph is unmistakeable. Is it pure coincidence? It is also to be remarked that the Greek historian, Herodotus, claims that AEsop the Storywriter was killed, so that atonement had to be made for his death.[8]

Then we may recall that in Part One we have encountered the *Book of Medicines*, associated with Asaph, son of Berechiah, which appeared around the ninth or tenth century and made reference to "the books of the wise men of India."[9] In *Barlaam and Joasaph* we also find a Barachias as the name of a Christian who came to the assistance of Joasaph and ultimately succeeded him as king of the Indian State.

So here we return to the Orient to continue our quest. The writer recalls one of the memorable sayings of Dr Inge, the Dean of St. Pauls, to this effect: "Wise Men came from the East to the cradle of the infant Christ. Is it not time that we paid them a return visit?"

## Chapter Two

# A Tomb in Kashmir

While the story of the Christian hero of *Barlaam and Joasaph* reflects that of the Buddha, we do not have to draw the conclusion that he was otherwise simply a creation of fiction. He could represent the tradition of someone else, someone who came to be linked with Jesus. In Eastern records we have circumstantial evidence that there had been such an individual.

We may take as an indication the Arabic edition of the Joasaph work published in Bombay under the title *Book of Balauhar and Budasaf*. The book closes with these words:

And he (Budasaf) reached Kashmir, and this was the most remote place in which he ministered, and there the end of his life overtook him. And he left the world, bequeathing his heritage to a certain disciple, Ababid by name, who served him and accompanied him; he was a man perfect in all his doings ... Afterwards he commanded Ababid to smooth out a place for him. Then he stretched out his legs and lay down; and he turned his head towards the north and his face to the east, and then he died.[1]

It has long been appreciated that a relationship clearly exists between the Budasaf (Joasaph) of the story and the mysterious saint and prophet Yus Asaph or Yuz-Asaf, whose tomb still exists,[2] and who is mentioned in many ancient records. He is remembered as *Shahzada Nabi* (The Prince Prophet).

One of the earliest accounts of Yuz-Asaf, if it can be relied upon, is given by Shaikh Al-Said-us-Sadiq in a work with a very long title, but commonly known as *Kamal-ud-din*. Al-Said is believed to have written some three hundred books, and to have died in 962 A.D. (A.H. 340). Once again we are in the tenth century. He speaks of the travels of Yuz-Asaf, and his eventual arrival in Kashmir, where he died. The account of his death is an obvious quotation of that of Budasaf, as given above. The disciple, however, is called Ba'bad, and the saint when dying stretches his legs towards the west and his head towards the east, which is more accurate.

The tomb of Yus Asaph (Yuz-Asaf) to which we are directed is at

Srinagar in Kashmir. The writer has not been able to ascertain the approximate date of the tomb on archaeological evidence, since the building over the tomb is sacred, and the tomb itself is in the crypt. It may be accepted to be of great antiquity but reliable ancient testimony is difficult to obtain for a variety of reasons. These include a lack of venerable manuscripts, differences in chronological systems in the East, the conversion of legends into statements of fact, and the insertion into old records of alterations and additions by copyists and translators to suit their own opinions. In particular – in our investigation – we have to note the influence on the traditions of the *Barlaam and Joasaph* book, where in the Christian version Joasaph is a disciple of Jesus, and no less the attempts to identify the mysterious prophet with Jesus himself.[4]

The tomb is located in the Khanyar district of Srinagar in a building called Rauzabal. There are two tombs which are on the ground floor in an inner chamber surrounded by a gallery, and these are visible through a carved lattice-work screen with openings. One of these tombs is nominally that of Yus Asaph, while the other is that of a devotee who lived much later than the prophet, named Syed Nasir-ud-Din Rizvi. These sepulchres are oriented north-south in accordance with Muslim custom. But the true tomb of Yus Asaph is in a crypt below, and this tomb is aligned east-west following Jewish custom so that the feet are pointed towards the Holy Land.

One of the most important clearly dated documents relating to the shrine is a certification granted to a former custodian Rahman Mir, entitling him to be the sole recipient of offerings made by visitors. The interesting thing about the text of this document is that it exhibits the influence of the *Barlaam and Joasaph* narrative, as well as furnishing other material information. We give the text in full.

In this Kingdom, in the Department of Learning and Piety and in the Court of Justice, Rahman Mir, son of Bahadur Mir, states that at the holy shrine of Yus-Asaf, prophet, may God bless him, nobles and ministers, kings and high dignitaries, and the general public, come from all directions to pay their homage and make offerings, and (he claims) that he is absolutely entitled to receive (and utilize) them; and no one else (has this right), and that all others should be restricted from (interfering with) his right.

After recording evidence it has been established that in the reign of Rajah Gopadatta who repaired the building on Mount Solomon and built many temples, a man came here whose name was Yuz-Asaf. He was a prince by descent, and had given up all wordly affairs, and was a lawgiver. He used to devote himself to prayer to God day and night; and used to spend most of his

time alone in meditation. This happened after the first great flood of
Kashmir when the people had taken to idol-worship. The Prophet Yuz-Asaf
had been sent as a prophet to preach to the people of Kashmir. He used to
proclaim the Unity of God till death overtook him and he died. He was
buried in Mohallah Khaniyar on the bank of the lake, (the place) which is
known as Rauzabal. In the year A.H.871 Syed Nasir-ud-din Rizvi, a
descendant of Imam Moosa Raza, was buried beside Yuz-Asaf.

Since the place is being visited regularly by all, high and low, and the said
Rahman Mir is the hereditary custodian of the place, he is entitled to receive
the offerings which may be made therein, and no one else has any right to or
connection with the said offerings.

Given under our hands this 11th Jumada-al-Thania 1184 A.H. Signed and
sealed:
> Mulla Faza, *Mufti-Azam*; Abdul Shakur, *Mufti-Azam*; Ahmadullah,
> *Mufti*; Muhammad Azam, *Mufti*; Hafiz Ahsanullahh, *Mufti*.

Signed and sealed:
> Muhammad Akbar, *Khadim*; Raza Akbar, *Khadim*; Khizar
> Muhammad, *Khadim*; Habibullah, *Khadim*.[5]

The information furnished by this legal decision is of considerable
importance. First of all it gives us two clear dates, and conveys a
third. We have the year when the official investigation took place,
namely 1184 A.H. (1806 A.D. of the Christian era). Then we have the
year of the death of the devotee whose body occupies the second of
the two upper tombs in the Rauzabal, namely 871 A.H. (1488 A.D.).
There must therefore by the fifteenth century have already for a
considerable time been a shrine here marking the tomb of Yuz-Asaf.
Finally, we have the opinion of the eighteenth century adjudicators,
that on the evidence before them it had been established to their
satisfaction that the prophet Yuz-Asaf had died in Kashmir in the
reign of Rajah Gopadatta.

Reliable evidence of the time in which Rajah Gopadatta was ruler
is not easy to obtain; but historians favour the second half of the first
century A.D. We shall need to return to this question later;[6] but wish
to consider here other points in the evidence of the certificate.

The testimony that Yuz-Asaf had been a prince who had surrendered his possessions in order to become a religious devotee answers
to what we find in the story of *Barlaam and Joasaph*, related to the life
of the Buddha. No other substantial testimony about Yuz-Asaf
would thus appear to have been available to the adjudicators when
they gave their ruling. But we have to remark that Yuz-Asaf is
presented as a real historical person, not a fictitious character. We are

in a chicken and egg position. Which came first? Is this a case of a legend historicised? Or has a real person been fictionalised? And if the latter, who was that person?

The questions come to mind but they have to be brushed aside while we pursue our researches. First we have to note here what is stated in the certification of the custodianship of the tomb. We have a positive reference to the repair of the building on Mount Solomon by Rajah Gopadatta in whose reign Yus-Asaf is said to have come to Kashmir. It is on record that in this building there were four inscriptions in Persian *Sulus* script. The first two were on two of the four pillars supporting the roof, while the others were on the side wall of the interior staircase. Al-Haj Khwaja Nazir Ahmad on pages 369 to 373 of his book, to which we have referred, deals with the evidence regarding these inscriptions.

One of those on the pillars commemorated the mason concerned with the construction, and was dated in the "Year Fifty and Four". It is this date we have to note, for it is the same as that given on the encasing walls with reference to Yuz-Asaf. The wall inscriptions are quoted as follows: (1) "At this time Yuz-Asaf proclaimed his prophethood. Year fifty and four," and (2) "He is Yusu, Prophet of the Children of Israel (*Bani Israil*)."

The inscriptions are quoted in a manuscript entitled *Tarikh-i-Kashmir* preserved at Srinagar, which is attributed to Mullah Nadiri, 832 A.H. (1444 A.D.), the earliest Muslim historian of Kashmir. There is corroborative reference to the four inscriptions, but only the one quoted in (1) above, relating to Yuz-Asaf, is confirmed verbally. Both the inscriptions on the wall have long been so mutilated as to be unreadable. This was already noted by Major H.H. Cole in his *Illustrations of Ancient Buildings in Kashmir* (London, 1869).

On the supposition that the inscriptions had been reported correctly by the fifteenth century author we have Yuz-Asaf identified with a Jewish prophet called Yusu. The name is rather like the common Hebrew contraction of Joseph to Jose,[7] which in Arabic would be from Yusuf to Yusu. But the proposal has been put forward strongly in modern times by the Ahmadiyya Movement that Yusu is actually Jesus, and that the tomb at Srinagar contains his remains.[8] Leaving this question aside for the present, we may observe that older historians do not appear to have been aware of such an identification, though in one instance the tomb is said to be that of a disciple of Jesus.

We give here some illustrations. Badi-ud-Din Abul Qasim was

writing in 1174 A.D. According to my source, he says of the tomb: "The assertion of the people of knowledge is that one of the disciples of Jesus (*yake as hawariyoon*) is buried there, from whose tomb emanates Divine grace and blessings."[9] This is interesting because, of course, the hero of *Barlaam and Josaphat* became a convert to Christianity.

Another manuscript in the name of Abdul Qadir dating from 1245 A.H. (1867 A.D.) states: "The tomb is described by the people of the locality as that of a prophet of the People of the Book (i.e the Jews)."[10] More precise is Mufti Ghulam Nabi Khanyari in his *Wajeez-ut-Tawarikh*, where we read:

The tomb of Syed Nasir-ud-Din is in Mohalla Khaniyar and is also known as Rauzabal. There is also the tomb of Yuz-Asaf, the prophet. He was a prince and had come to this place. Through prayers and (because of his) piety he had come as a Messenger to the people of Kashmir, and he preached to them. It is said that at that time Rajah Gopadatta was the ruler. There was a hole (aperture) in the western wall (of the tomb) out of which aroma of musk used to emanate. A woman with an infant child came to pay her respects. The child passed urine into the hole. The woman became insane."

Finally we come to one of the most distinguished historians of Kashmir named Khwaja Muhammad Azam of Deedamari. He completed his work *Waqiat-i-Kashmir* (alternatively known as *Tarikh-i-Azami*) in 1148 A.H. (1770 A.D.).[11] The author has this to say about the Rauzabal:

Besides that grave (i.e. of Syed Nasir-ud-din) there is a tomb. It is well known amongst the people of the locality that there lies a prophet who had come to Kashmir in ancient times. It is now known as the place of the Prophet. I have seen in a book of history that (he had come) after great tribulations from a great distance. It is said that a prince, after undergoing a good deal of penance and perseverance and through devotion and prayers had become the Messenger of God to the people of Kashmir. On reaching Kashmir he invited people (to his religion) and after death was laid to rest in Anzmarah. In this book the name of the Prophet is given as Yuz-Asaf. Anzmarah is in Khaniyar. Many pious people, and especially the spiritual guide of the author: Mullah Inayiatullah Shaul, say that while visiting the tomb Divine grace and blessings of prophethood were witnessed."

Had the authorities quoted here identified the tomb of Yuz-Asaf with that of the famed Jesus, an exalted figure in Islam, they would certainly have featured a matter of such importance. Their silence is eloquent. It is not disputed that this was proposed in the late nineteenth century. And we have to appreciate that accounts of the life and teaching of Jesus and of the Buddha did get interwoven in the East in the early Christian centuries following the arrival of missionaries. Certain parables are ascribed to both, and we have particularly been concerned with the part played by the spread of the tale of *Barlaam and Joasaph*.

However it needs to be stated that Professor F.M. Hassnain, Head of the Department of Archaeology at Srinagar found at the tomb on a slab used as a base for candles, and under deposits of candle wax, a crucifix and also a rosary. On the stone itself were carvings which appeared to be of the soles of two feet bearing nail wounds. These remains at least testified that Christians were among the many visitors to the tomb over a number of centuries, which would be quite appropriate if there was familiarity with the *Barlaam and Joasaph* story which in its Christian content had claimed Joasaph (Josaphat) as a great Christian saint to whom a holy day in the calendar had been assigned.[12] The relics themselves, crucifix and rosary, could not be earlier than the Middle Ages, and of course no orthodox Christian, believing Jesus to be in heaven, could possibly have entertained the idea that his body was interred at Srinagar.

## Chapter Three

# Light from the East

There is an important source to which we have not yet referred, but which must not be omitted. It is a Hindu work entitled *Bhavishya Maha Purana*, which is written in Sanskrit by one called Sutta, and claimed to date from 115A.D. This was printed and published for the first time in 1910 in a translation made by Vidyavaridi Dr Shiv Nath Shastri under the sponsorship of H.H. Maharajah Sir Partap Singh of Kashmir.[1] In the following quotation I have placed within square brackets a short passage which is somewhat dittographic and in all probability an interpolation.

The Sakas came to Aryadesh (India) after crossing the Indus and some (came) through other routes in the Himalayas, and started plundering the place. After some time some of them left and took back (with them) their booty. Some time after Rajah Shalewahin succeeded to the throne. He in a very short time defeated the Sakas, Chinese, Tartars, Walhiks (i.e. Bokharis), Kamrups (i.e. Parthians) and Khurasanis and punished them. Then he put the *maleech* (i.e. infidels) and Aryas in separate countries. The *maleech* were kept up to the Indus river (on the far side) and the Aryas on this side. One day he went to a country in the Himalayas. There he saw (what appeared to be) a Rajah of Sakas at Wien,[2] who was fair in colour and wore white clothes. He (Shalewahin) asked (him) who he was. His reply was that he was *Yusashaphat* (i.e. Josaphat), and had been born of a woman, and he said that he spoke the truth and he had to purify the religion. The Rajah asked him what his religion was. He replied, 'O Rajah, when truth had disappeared and there was no limit (to the evil practices) in the *maleech* country, I appeared there and through my work the guilty and the wicked suffered, and I also suffered at their hands.' [The Rajah asked him what his religion was. He replied, 'It is love, truth, and purity of heart, and for this I am called *Isa Masih* (i.e. Jesus Christ).'] The Rajah returned after making obeisance to him . . .

There are difficulties about the authority of this text, though it has some traditional value. The prophet names himself as Yusashaphat, which is interesting, comparable to the Hebrew Jehoshaphat, and recalling the western spelling of Joasaph as Josaphat. But later he gives his name as Isa Masih. I propose to treat this passage as an interpolation for several reasons. First the prophet had already stated his name as Yusashaphat, second the Rajah asked him what his religion was when he had previously asked the very same question and had been answered and thirdly he gives his name the second time as Isa Masih, the Muslim Arabic version of Jesus Christ, and this in a book claiming to date long before Islam, from the second century A.D., written in Sanskrit by a Hindu.

We must now seek to draw together some of the threads from our oriental carpet. We begin by noting certain matters which do not directly tie in with anything in the *Barlaam and Joasaph* literature, but do suggest an Essene derivation. Thus in the document from which we have just quoted the mysterious person whom the Rajah encounters is said to wear a white robe, which was the practice of the Essenes. In his own country he had challenged the evildoers and had suffered at their hands. This was the case with the True Teacher. The orthodox rabbis of the second century regarded the wearing of white garments as one of the marks of a Jewish heretic or sectarian, and those who were thus attired were not permitted to lead the prayers in the synagogue.[3]

In the previous chapter [4] we gave an excerpt from the *Waqiat-i-Kashmir* of Khwaja Muhammad Azam of Deedamari. In the same work the author says that Yuz-Asaf was a descendant of Moses, which means that he was of the priestly tribe of Levi, again like the True Teacher of the Essenes. He could not therefore be identical with Jesus, who was descended from King David of the tribe of Judah. In the custodian certificate associated with the tomb of Yuz-Asaf, quoted above p.99, the prophet is also called a lawgiver, which was the status of the True Teacher.

While attempts have been made, no good reason has been given by anyone why, if Jesus was the prophet concerned, he should have adopted such a name as Yus Asaph (Yuz-Asaf), or wished to do so. Linguistically there is no connection between the two names; but there is an obvious connection with the Joseph-Asaph representation of the True Teacher.

The Eastern writers have not been in a position to be aware of the Joseph-Asaph traditions, since knowledge that such an individual as the True Teacher had existed among the Jews had almost completely disappeared. It required the chance discovery of the Dead Sea Scrolls to resurrect him. So it has not previously been practicable to have him, and the legacy he left, in mind when investigating the Yus Asaph records.

In Part One of this book, chapters five and seven especially, we were able to make contact with the Messianic heritage relating to the True Teacher through the appropriated names of Joseph and Asaph. We also noted, in this context,[5] the special significance given to the name Joseph in the Biblical psalms credited to Asaph, where Joseph is peculiarly identified with the tribes of Israel, and in one place the name is written in Hebrew as Jehoseph. There is a curious link between *Psalm* lxxx.1 (an Asaph psalm) and the blessing on the Patriarch Joseph in *Genesis* xlix.22-24. In the former, verse one, we read: "Give ear, O Shepherd of Israel, Thou that leadest Joseph (i.e. the tribes of Israel) like a flock." In the latter, Joseph (i.e. the Patriarch) is described as a sufferer, but who was "made strong by the hands of the Mighty One of Jacob; (from thence is the shepherd, the stone of Israel).

There have been a great many endeavours in the past to seek out evidence in the East of what became of the Ten Tribes of Israel who were, at least in part, carried away captive by the Assyrians, in the eighth century B.C., when they conquered the Northern Kingdom of Israel. Evidences from many sources, East and West, were assembled, for instance, by Hazrat Mirza Ghulam Ahmad of Qadian in his book *Masih Hindustan Mein* at the close of the nineteenth century.[6] The aim of that book, englished as *Jesus in India*, was to confirm the claim that Jesus had escaped death on the cross, and later had travelled to the East to preach to the Lost Ten Tribes of Israel. These were to be found, it was affirmed, in Afghanistan and Kashmir, where they had migrated. Eventually Jesus had reached there after his resurrection, where finally he had died and was buried at Srinagar at the advanced age of 125. The tomb of Yus Asaph was claimed as his.

With the question of whether Jesus went to India we are not at present concerned, except to note that there became attached to him the reputation of being an inveterate traveller, who could – as has been suggested – be the original of the Wandering Jew.[7]

More immediately we are to think of the Wandering Jews; for the information furnished in the oriental sources does not clearly distinguish between the two captivities, of Israel and of Judah respectively. They commonly refer to the conquest in the sixth century B.C. of the Southern Kingdom of Judah and its capital, Jerusalem, by Nebuchadnezzar, and the captivity from there of the tribes of Judah and Benjamin. They link these circumstances with the fate of the Ten Tribes of the Northern Kingdom of Israel as if they were one and the same event.

This error has great significance, because it shows that it is not what happened to the Ten Tribes which matters so much as the circumstances relating to much later eastward movements of Jewish groups and sects down to the middle of the first millennium A.D., and beginning in the days of the Medo-Persian Empire. It is not ruled out that some remnants of the captives from the Northern Kingdom of Israel may have persisted as distinct clans. But it is much more probable that the pockets of Jews, or persons of Jewish descent, to be found in the East at the time of the spread of Islam, would tend to claim a relationship with the lost tribes as a matter of prestige or folklore though factually this did not exist.

We have also to bear in mind that many from the Northern Kingdom became integrated with the Southern Kingdom both before and after the Babylonian Exile; so that the Jewish People[8] at the time of Christ could and did, quite properly describe themselves as the Children of Israel, and their country as the Land of Israel. Jesus would have had no need to go outside his own country to seek lost sheep of the House of Israel. He was, of course, concerned in this respect with individuals. He did not claim to be seeking lost tribes.

Among eastern contenders to represent the Lost Ten Tribes the Afghans have had pride of place. They have long thought of themselves as related to the Bani Israel, (Children of Israel) and European travellers from the 18th century onward have commented on their Jewish features and certain customs. One of their clans noted in this respect is called Yusuf-Zai (the Joseph clan). J.P. Ferrier records in his *History of the Afghans* (1858 A.D.), that when Nadir Shah was marching to the conquest of India, and had reached Peshawar, the chief of this clan "presented him with a Bible written in Hebrew, and several other articles that had been used in their ancient worship, and which they had preserved. These articles were at once recognised by the Jews who followed the camp."

While, since the coming of Islam, the Yusuf-Zai have been inclined to dissociate themselves from the Jews, the references to their origins – those of the Afghans – link them particularly with the tribes which were *not* lost, those of Judah and Benjamin, dating their eastward movement to the destruction of Jerusalem and the Jewish Temple there. The writer has been able to find no records of the capture of Samaria, the capital of the Kingdom of Israel, in the Afghan and

Kashmiri traditions, which would be appropriate if the Ten Tribes were concerned. We are reminded that the actual tomb of Yus Asaph at Srinagar is oriented with the feet towards the West,[9] following the custom of Jews and Judaeo-Christians in the East, who held Jerusalem to be sacred and its Temple to be the House of God.

The question then arises, what would have driven Jews – and especially Jewish sectarians, such as the Essenes and Nazoreans – to trek eastward? The answer must surely be what is indicated by tradition, the defeat of the Jews in A.D.70, and the circumstances preceding the war with the Romans.

We are familiar, from Christian sources, with the flight of the Nazoreans to Transjordan just before the war, and there was the abandonment by the Essenes of their major community at Qumran due to the same circumstances. Earlier persecutions of Christians and Mandaeans in Judaea had necessitated the escape of many to the north-east, and onward to Mesopotamia where they could gain asylum.

Again the stories relating to Yus-Asaph (Joasaph) furnish some confirmation. He is said to have come to Kashmir in the reign of Rajah Gopadatta. That monarch is said to have ruled for sixty years, from approximately 49 to 109 A.D. At the beginning of this chapter we reported the tradition that Joasaph had been encountered in Kashmir by Rajah Shalewahin, who seems to have left Kashmir around 78 A.D. This would correspond with the year 3154 of the Laukika era, according to the calculations of Al-Haj Khwaja Nazir Ahmad, possibly accounting for the number 54 in the inscriptions on the building on Mount Solomon.[10]

The chronological evidence is not conclusive, as we have pointed out, because of the different eras used in the East and the uncertainty of the historical references. But there is at least a chance that the tribulations in Palestine of those of The Way had a connection with the claimed arrival of Yus-Asaph in Kashmir.

Everything we have so far considered in the oriental records relating to this personality is distinctively Essene, and linked with their Joseph-Asaph exegesis. And at this point, therefore, we should introduce certain traditions regarding the origin of the Afghans.

The sources are somewhat confused, but they are remarkable. These have to do with the belief that the progenitor of the Afghans was Malik Talut (King Saul in the Bible). He, of course, was from the tribe of Benjamin, which was certainly not one of the Lost Ten

Tribes. Talut, it is said, had two sons. The views that agree say that their names were Barkhiya (Berechiah) and Armijah (Jeremiah). Barkhija was the father of Asaf, who built Solomon's temple, and Armijah had a son called Afghana. Afghana, from whom sprang the Afghans, was thus the cousin of Asaph son of Berechiah. The descendants of Afghana were carried captive to Babylon by King Nebuchadnezzar, who later removed them to the mountains of Ghore in Afghanistan.[11]

The names of Berechiah, and of course the Prophet Jeremiah, have a relationship with the reasons for the capture of Jerusalem by Nebuchadnezzar.[12] And the Jewish tribulation of those days, as we have illustrated in Part One, was regarded as a judgment on the Jews for apostasy, repeated in the time of Antiochus Epiphanes, and again in the time of Vespasian.

But the appearance at all of the famed Asaph ben Berechiah in an Afghan context is startling, as is that of Jeremiah. It only makes sense if the legends reflected contact with Essene sources.

*Chapter Four*

# The Wandering Jew

In the oriental texts Yus Asaph comes before us as a refugee from evildoers and evil deeds, rather than as a missionary seeking to spread a gospel. Jesus in certain Muslim records is similarly represented. This had been noted by the founder of the Ahmadiyya Movement in *Jesus in India*. He quoted certain Muslim *Hadith* pronouncements from *Kanz-ul-Ummal*. "A *Hadith* from Abu Huraira: God directed Jesus (on whom be peace), 'O Jesus! Move from one place to another' – go from one country to another lest thou shouldst be recognised and persecuted." He also quotes from the same source, on the report of Jabar, the *Hadith* that Jesus used to travel from one country to another, subsisting only on vegetation and pure water. Another report has it, on the authority of Abdullah bin–Umar that when the Holy Prophet had stated that the poor are most favoured in God's sight, he was asked, "Were they the people who, like Jesus the Messiah, fled from their country with their faith?" The travel stories are here in connection with Jesus, venerated by Muslims, rather than with the mysterious Yus Asaph; but the hero is still a refugee from persecution and not a missionary.[1]

In a Paper read at the International Conference on The Deliverance of Jesus from the Cross, held in London in 1978,[2] Dr Ladislav Filip suggested that conceivably Jesus as the 'Travelling Jew' might be the original on whom was afterwards constructed by Christians antagonistic to the Jews the legend of the Wandering Jew.

What is known of this legend? As it was represented in the seventeenth century the legend related to a Jew named Ahasuerus, who had taunted Jesus on his way to crucifixion, and was told by him, "Go on for ever till I return." As a result various persons through the centuries claimed to have encountered this person, who could not die. But the original story had to do with a Jew who was friendly to Jesus, namely Joseph of Arimathaea, and was somewhat similar to what is recorded in John's Gospel concerning the Beloved Disciple. Jesus had told Peter regarding him, "If I will that he tarry till I come, what is that to thee". And the passage continues: "Then went this saying abroad among the brethren that this disciple should not die" (Jn.xxi.21–23).

The earliest reference to Joseph of Arimathaea that I have been able to trace in this connection is in the *Flores Historiarum* of Roger de Wendover, dating from 1228 A.D. But evidently there was already at that time a tradition in Christian circles relating to the longevity of Joseph. Roger relates that when an archbishop from Armenia was visiting the Abbey of St. Albans in England the monks questioned him about Joseph of Arimathaea. The archbishop told them that Joseph was certainly alive, and that he had encountered him; but he was known as Joseph Cartaphilus. Joseph of Arimathaea had urged Jesus forward on his way to crucifixion, and Jesus had said to him, "I go, but thou shalt wait till I come."

It is significant that the legend should be linked with an eastern area like Armenia, for Armenian was one of the languages into which Essene literature was translated in the early Christian centuries, and also with the name Joseph. It is also important it should embrace the idea of a wanderer from land to land, as reported in oriental tradition regarding Yus Asaph and Jesus.

But should we not go back to the Joseph-Asaph material of the Essenes relating to the True Teacher? In this tradition the Teacher's life is threatened; but, at least initially, he is miraculously preserved and makes good his escape abroad. The *Thanksgiving Psalms* found among the Dead Sea Scrolls have been held in large part to have been his compositions and to reflect his experiences. We may repeat here part of what we have already quoted from Psalm 7 of this collection. "They have banished me from my land like a bird from its nest; all my friends and brethren are driven far from me, and hold me for a broken vessel."[3]

There is another collection of ancient poems known as the *Odes of Solomon*, which also has a bearing on the circumstances. The contents of this work are very mixed, Judaeo-Christian and Gnostic, and having some Essene affiliations. One of the Odes is in fact directly related to the Essene *Thanksgiving Psalms*, and opens as they do with the words, "I thank Thee, O Lord." We give here Dr J. Rendel Harris's translation from the Syriac.[4]

I will give thanks unto Thee, O Lord, because I love Thee. O Most High, Thou wilt not forsake me, for Thou art my hope. Freely I have received Thy grace: I shall live thereby. My persecutors will come and not see me: a cloud of darkness shall fall on their eyes; and an air of thick gloom shall darken them; and they shall have no light to see: that they may not take hold of me. Let their counsel become thick darkness, and what they have cunningly devised, let it return upon their own heads. For they have devised a counsel, and it did not succeed: they have prepared themselves for evil, and were found to be empty. For my hope is upon the Lord, and I will not fear, and because the Lord is my salvation, I will not fear: and He is as a garland upon my head and I shall not be moved; even if everything should be shaken, I stand firm; and if all things visible should perish, I shall not die; because the Lord is with me, and I am with Him. Hallelujah.

Not only is the True Teacher forced to leave his country because of persecution, there is also an attempt by his enemies to have him pursued and assassinated. This plan fails, and the Teacher makes good his escape. He is confident now that he will not perish, and rather grandiosely affirms: "If all things visible should perish, I shall not die."

Thus, nearly two hundred years before the ministry of Jesus, there had been the experiences of the True Teacher, who like the Patriarch Joseph, had been hated by his brethren and had narrowly escaped death at their hands. In the Essene scheme of things there would be a manifestation of the True Teacher in the Last Times, a circumstance which his followers applied to Jesus as we can see in the Christian interpolations in the *Testaments of the Twelve Patriarchs*, and in references to him as the True Prophet in the *Clementine* literature.[5] Jesus was a son of Joseph, and we have the messianic concepts of a suffering Messiah Ben Joseph. There was, therefore, some justification for linking Joasaph with Jesus, especially as the latter was so well known to Muslims.

There would also be the possibility that some Christians, learning of the Joseph (Joasaph) tales, would attach them to Joseph of Arimathaea, who was believed to have escaped from Palestine, because the chief priests were concerned as to what part he had played in the disappearance of the body of Jesus from the tomb. Most readers will be familiar with the legend that Joseph of Arimathaea reached Britain where he deposited the crown of thorns at Glastonbury, which grew into a tree.

It is even conceivable that the singular could give rise to the collective, or at least endorse it. We have seen in an Asaph psalm how the name Joseph had come to be applied to the people of Israel as a whole.[6] Jewish refugees who found asylum in Afghanistan could thus give rise to the Yusuf-Zai (Joseph clan).[7]

We have traced westward movements also, notably around the twelfth century. We have made reference to the Bogomil wandering apostles. But of particular note are those described by Catholic Councils as "*circumcisos, passaginos, Josephinos*".[8] These Josephists, whoever they were, belonged to a sect which was Jewish and migrant.

While we are in an area of speculation here we may think of the name Cartaphilus, said by the Armenians to have been adopted by the Wandering Jew Joseph. The surname suggests card-lover. Jews are well-known lovers of card games, and conceivably there may be some connection with fortune-telling by cards, cartomancy. Playing cards seem to have been introduced into Europe from Arab lands in the thirteenth century. The Spanish name *Naipes* and the Italian *Naibi*, suggests prediction, and may derive from the Hebrew for a prophet *Nabi*, which in Arabic is *Nebi*. With the *Tarot* the fortune-telling pack consists of 22 cards, the same number as the letters of the Hebrew alphabet. Is there a link with those wanderers from the East, the Gypsies?

We pose these questions because we have to entertain many possibilities in hope that among them will be found profitable clues, especially in the association of names and traditions.

As a pointer in the direction we seek to travel we have several times encountered both the historical and legendary links between the Biblical Asaph ben Berechiah and the famed King Solomon. Like this monarch Asaph is depicted in Jewish and Islamic folklore as a master of the occult.[9] We should therefore at this stage develop the Solomonic aspect of our quest.

## Chapter Five

# The Sun King

King Solomon of Bible fame and folk fable comes before us by tradition as the ancestor and archetype of the Davidic Messiah. He is by name the Prince of Peace (*Shelomo*) and also by repute, and by adoption Son of God (*Ps.*ii), one upon whom has been conferred wisdom and understanding, counsel and might.[1] The Prophet Nathan predicted to King David:

I will set up thy seed after thee, which shall proceed out of thy bowels, and I will establish his kingdom. He shall build an house for My Name, and I will establish the throne of his kingdom for ever. I will be his father, and he shall be My son. If he commit iniquity, I will chasten him with the rod of men . . . But My mercy shall not depart away from him . . . And thine house and thy kingdom shall be established for ever before thee: thy throne shall be established for ever" (*II.Sam* vii.12-14).

In course of time Solomon became a legendary figure, the wisest man who ever lived, master of magic and the secret arts, whom even the demons must obey, as they would obey his descendant Jesus. Books were written about him and named after him, and his person and rule were seen as anticipations of the ultimate Messianic Kingdom.

A Jewish passage introduced into the *Sibylline Oracles* declares of the ultimate Jewish ruler: "And then shall God send from the sun a king who shall make all the earth cease from ruinous war . . . And the Temple of the high God shall be loaded with rich adornments, the gold and silver and furnishings of purple; and the fruitful earth and sea shall abound in good things."[2]

The Messiah here reflects Solomon as the Sun King, the guise in which he is depicted by the historian Josephus. In his pages we see the monarch sitting high in his chariot attended by his mounted bodyguard.

The riders, in the first flower of a youth that was most delightful to see, and of a conspicuous height, were much taller than other men; they let their hair down to a very great length and were dressed in tunics of Tyrian purple. And every day they sprinkled their hair with gold dust so that their heads sparkled as the gleam of the gold was reflected by the sun. With these men about him . . . the king himself was accustomed to mount his chariot, clothed with a white garment, and go out for a ride.[3]

Here Solomon in his brilliant white robe is the sun, surrounded by youths whose gold-sprinkled tresses represent its rays. The association was taken up by the Essenes, as Josephus also reports, who prayed daily towards the east as though beseeching the sun to rise.[4] The Essene practice was followed by the early Christians, who – according to Pliny the Younger – "met on a fixed day before it was light, and sang an antiphonal chant to Christ, as if to a god."[5] We also find Paul quoting from some hymn,[6]

> "Rouse yourself, sleeper,
> And arise from the dead,
> And Christ shall shine on you."

Jesus himself could speak of the Sun King as "Solomon in all his glory."[7]

There are ingredients in the Biblical account of Solomon which made their appeal to the Essenes. These relate to the Temple and the Priesthood. Solomon had been anointed king by the priest Zadok, whose descendants – according to the prediction of the prophet Ezekiel – would serve in the ultimate Sanctuary of the Messianic Age.

But the priests the Levites, the Sons of Zadok, that kept the charge of My sanctuary when the children of Israel went astray from Me, they shall come near to Me to minister unto Me, and they shall stand before Me to offer unto Me the fat and the blood, saith the Lord God . . . And it shall come to pass, that when they enter in at the gates of the inner court, they shall be clothed with linen garments; and no wool shall come upon them, whiles they minister in the gates of the inner court, and within.[8]

It would appear that one of the Essene documents was a *Book of Zadok*, and among the finds near their community centre at Qumran was a copper scroll listing the location of buried treasures. Included among them were vessels for incense hidden "below the southern corner of the portico at Zadok's tomb and underneath the pilaster in the exedras." One of the recovered Essene works from Qumran has been the remarkable *Temple Scroll*.

The Essenes used the passage we have quoted from *Ezekiel* to distinguish three stages in their history: the 'priests' were their initial emigrants from Judaea, the 'levites' were those who joined them, and the faithful at the End of Days are termed 'sons of Zadok'.[9] The name of Zadok the Priest is still linked with the anointing of British monarchs at the coronation ceremony, which is based on that of Solomon.

We have already observed how the Afghans claimed descent from Afghana, whose cousin Asaph had built the temple of Solomon.[10] Architects and other visitors to Kashmir have pointed out the likeness of temples there to the plan of the temple at Jerusalem. For example, G.T. Vigne has written:[11] "I had been struck with the great resemblance which the temples bore to the recorded disposition of the Ark, and its surrounding curtains, and in imitation of which the temple at Jerusalem was built: and it became for a moment a question whether the Kashmirian temples had not been built by Jewish architects."

Another writer, dealing with the temple at Martand in Kashmir, has remarked: "But it is one of the points of interest in the Kashmir temples that they reproduce, in plan at least, the Jewish temple, more nearly than any other building."[12]

In the neighbourhood of Srinagar, where the tomb of Yus Asaph is situated, there is another building to which we have already referred,[13] a temple built on Mount Solomon, known as *Takht-i-Sulaiman*. I have not been able to verify this, but Al-Haj Khwaja Nazir Ahmad claimed that this was an exact replica of the building outside Jerusalem commonly known as the Tomb of Absalom. Local legend in Kashmir has it that King Solomon, as skilled a magician as Asaph his contemporary, landed here on one of his aerial excursions, being, as the Quran tells, a master of the winds.

All that we have adduced in this chapter does not, perhaps, amount to a great deal evidentially. Islamic sources in particular love to identify tales of holy and famous persons with particular places, around which legends are woven. The Catholic Church has been noted for a similar exercise of creative imagination. Both religions, for example, are interested in the imagined experiences of the Holy Family in Egypt. We have therefore to be careful not to put two and two together and make five. But there may just be something in the traditions that has picked up and developed elements of an Essene heritage.

There was a mystical lore attaching to the Solomonic Temple not only in the East. It reached Europe in the Middle Ages to find a repository among the arcane secrets of the Templars and Freemasons.

### Chapter Six

# Did Jesus Survive?

At various points in our search we have encountered the view that the Yus-Asaph to whom the tomb at Srinagar is ascribed was in reality Jesus under an assumed name, or one conferred upon him. The arguments in support of this opinion can adduce one or two testimonies that are favourable. But mostly those who advocate it do not handle their evidences very carefully and jump too readily to conclusions. In some instances wishful thinking and special pleading are very obvious. Admittedly a good many of the available resources are unsatisfactory and highly speculative; but one must apply, as far as is practicable, judgements that are open-minded and governed by scientific methods.

While seeking to introduce whatever material may be relevant and illuminating, and exploring the pointers in particular directions, we have so far taken very few positive positions. We have not yet come to an end of our resources, but we have now reached the stage when certain issues can be brought to a head. The first of these is very clear. Whatever may be the true explanation of the circumstances, the prophet who in ancient times resided for many years in Kashmir and was buried there cannot conceivably be identical with Jesus of Nazareth, unless the latter did not die by crucifixion at Jerusalem as Christianity has represented, or, having risen from the dead, as also affirmed by the Church, thereafter resumed normal physical existence on earth.

The issue is clear cut. Jesus and Yus-Asaph cannot be one and the same if Jesus went to heaven and remained there, or if on earth he failed to recover from the ordeal of the cross. They could theoretically be identical if someone else at Jerusalem was crucified in place of Jesus, or if his body was taken secretly from the tomb and given treatment that resulted in his full recovery.

The theoretical positions, if demonstrable, would not amount to any kind of proof that Jesus and Yus-Asaph were the same man, but without the survival of Jesus on earth the supposed or proposed identification does not arise at all.

But before we approach the question of the survival of Jesus in this world let us look again at the view that Jesus must have travelled to the East in order to proclaim his message to the Lost Ten Tribes of Israel. This appears to the writer to be a rather wilful misinterpretation of the Gospels, unwarranted special pleading in support of a theory.

In the New Testament the Holy Land is clearly described as the "Land of Israel" (*Mt*.ii.20-21) and its inhabitants are called "Israel" (*Mt*.viii.10). Jesus declared that he was sent to the "lost *sheep* of the house of Israel" (*Mt*.xv.24), that is, sheep who because of sin had gone astray, not tribes which had disappeared. Further, he instructed his apostles not to go to any Gentile areas or any Samaritan city (*Mt*.x.5). He himself, as Messiah designate of Israel, never throughout his ministry departed from his own instructions, travelling only within the geographical limits of the Land of Israel, and never entering a Gentile house or city. Consequently it was quite contrary to his understanding of his Messianic function as King of Israel that he should travel to distant lands or proclaim his message to non-Jews.

When the Gospels were written circumstances had radically changed, and in many lands individuals of many nationalities had joined the Church. Therefore there was added an instruction of Jesus (as risen from the dead) that his followers should proclaim the gospel to all mankind. That Jesus had said nothing of the kind is clear from the *Acts of the Apostles*, where it is agreed that the disciples, in accordance with the teaching they had received from Jesus, preached initially only to Jews (*Acts* xi.19), and Peter was criticised for visiting the home even of a God-fearing Gentile (*Acts* xi.3).

We may therefore rule out the possibility that, if Jesus should have travelled to eastern lands, it was because of some general missionary obligations or to contact Israel's lost tribes. The evidences we have produced are all to the same effect, that it is the fall of Judaea and Jersusalem that is recalled in Eastern traditions, not the fall of the northern kingdom of Israel and its capital Samaria.[1] The Yus-Asaph stories relate to a Jewish refugee, not to a Christian missionary.

But to have gone to the remote East for any reason at all Jesus must have been in a physical condition fit for such arduous travel from land to land. Accordingly, he must either not have been crucified, or have recovered from the effects of crucifixion by a miraculous resurrection from the dead, or have had the opportunity for the perfect healing of his wounds.

The earliest evidences we have are all agreed that Jesus was crucified. Docetic and Gnostic ideas, which would deny him this physical experience, have their basis in doctrinal concepts of the sinfulness of the flesh regardless of the historical circumstances. Those who cite secondary and sectarian sources of evidence have to use great caution in their employment of such records. We may therefore ignore all such ideas as that the body which suffered on the cross only appeared to be that of Jesus, or that someone else was made to look like him and suffered in his stead.

The orthodox Christian testimony, that Jesus died on the cross, and after his entombment was subsequently in a miraculous manner raised from the dead and restored to physical life, is in line with Jewish notions. But, as the sources convey when analysed, faith has tampered with historical evidences, calling not only for a resurrection with the presence of angels, but also for a subsequent ascension to heaven. These two circumstances are interrelated. There is no proposition that Jesus having been raised from the dead, resumed normal active existence on earth for a great many years. The accounts given of the Early Church in the New Testament find no place for his movements and activities in the decades following his restoration to life. It is claimed that he was carried up to heaven, and would only return at some indefinite date in the future (*Acts* i.10-11). The Christian viewpoint, therefore, provides no warrant for the assumption that Jesus continued on earth for a protracted period, able to travel to the East, and even to marry and beget children.

There remains another possibility, which is in harmony with certain indications in the Gospels, and that is that Jesus was still alive when he was released from the cross. He was hastily laid in a tomb which was above ground. This view would hold with a design to re-enter the tomb at the earliest opportunity after the conclusion of the Sabbath, for the purpose of conveying Jesus elsewhere for skilled medical treatment that, hopefully, would result in his recovery.[2]

It was practicable, and it is on record, that the life of someone crucified could be saved if circumstances were favourable and expert aid could be given very quickly. We do not, unfortunately, have evidence of the physical and mental condition of such survivors. They would be likely to be permanently crippled to some extent, and there would be a risk of some brain damage, depending on how long the victim had been on the cross. With Jesus, because he had been crucified on the eve of the Sabbath, his ordeal – as the Gospels indicate – had been unusually short. The two others who had been crucified with him at the same time were still living when sunset approached on Friday evening, and accordingly their legs were broken, as was customary, to expedite death. Jesus himself was evidently unconscious, but not necessarily dead. It is related that to make sure he did die a Roman soldier pierced his side with a spear. Either the infliction of this wound was successful, or it very seriously reduced his chances of recovery, even if his body came very quickly into friendly and skilled hands.

It has been argued that there was a plan to preserve Jesus through the agency of Joseph of Arimathaea and his associates, a possibility which the Gospel accounts would allow. Because of his influential status Joseph was able to obtain permission from the Roman governor to receive immediately the body of Jesus before sunset on the day of the crucifixion. Spices and clean linen had been brought which would be antiseptic and help to staunch the wounds, and Jesus had been immediately conveyed to an adjacent tomb which was above ground and ventilated. This could have been a temporary measure until the Sabbath had ended; but it was obviously of the utmost consequence that the body of Jesus should not be flung into the ground by his executioners, when survival would have been impossible. The opened entrance of the sepulchre, with the disappearance of the body and the discarded wrappings as discovered early on Sunday morning, could mean that an attempt had been made to save Jesus. The one, or more men dressed in white seen by the women who came to perform offices for the dead could have been Essenes rather than angels. Their presence would tend to support the view that the recovery of Jesus was planned, since the Essenes would be on his side and were skilled doctors.

If this interpretation of the circumstances is correct, Jesus would necessarily have been conveyed in the night to some reliable hide-out for the protracted treatment that would have been essential. There could be no question of an almost spontaneous restoration of active life. He would have been incapable of the recorded immediate appearance to various disciples, or of making the long journey to Galilee shortly after. What is more he would have been without clothing.

Reliable evidence is lacking that Jesus as a human being recovered from the experience of crucifixion and resumed normal existence. The assumption is therefore appropriate that after he was brought out of the tomb either he was found to have expired, or that he died shortly after. There could be no question of returning the body to the tomb and reclosing the entrance. Those concerned dare not linger. The risk of discovery was too great. In the circumstances only one thing was practicable – to convey the body to some wilderness spot and bury it in secret. Of such an event the immediate disciples of Jesus would be totally unaware, as the plan to rescue him would be unsafe if entrusted to them. Indeed, as tradition records, they were in all probability in hiding themselves as militant Galileans. The chief factor in the failure of the plan would have been the fact that the spear wound in the side of Jesus had not been anticipated.

The view expressed here would provide a natural explanation of the discovery on Sunday morning that the tomb was empty with the wrappings of the body discarded. The words of Mary Magdalene ring true when she reported to Peter, "They have taken the Master out of the sepulchre and we don't know where they have put him" (*Jn*.xx.2). *They* might be thought to be enemies rather than friends, a case of grave robbery or a precautionary action on the part of the authorities. Since this would be the natural conclusion, it is quite consistent that a man in white – an Essene – would be left in the vicinity to reassure the visiting women that no persons hostile to Jesus had been responsible.

An alternative proposition has been put forward by Hazrat Ghulam Ahmad of Qadian, namely that the wounds of Jesus healed in a matter of days. This is attributed to the action of a salve referred to in many old medical treatises, and called *Marham-i-Isa* (Ointment of Jesus). It is claimed that this ointment was either invented by Jesus, or was available – presumably from the Essenes – and employed for his wounds.[3] To quote this author: "Within three days he (Jesus) recovered sufficiently to be able to march seventy miles on foot from Jerusalem to Galilee."

Customarily it had been presumed, in accordance with John's Gospel (xi.44, xix.40), that the body of Jesus when laid in the tomb had been wound round and round with a linen cloth in which spices had been placed in the folds. There is no hint of any ointment here. Of course, it could have been applied after the body of Jesus had been unwrapped and removed from the tomb. But that would argue in favour of the rescue theory. Various papers, appropriate to the theme of the survival of Jesus, were read in 1978 in London at an International Conference organized by the Ahamdiyya Movement on the theme of "The Deliverance of Jesus from the Cross." At this Conference, however, the view was not brought forward that there had been a prearranged plan to enable Jesus to survive crucifixion.

To most of the propositions which were presented to the conference there has been allusion at various places in this work. But one of them has been reserved until this point, and that is the evidence of the Turin Shroud, held by many to be the actual cloth which covered the body of Jesus in the tomb, and which bears in negative likeness the imprint of the front and back of a bearded man who had apparently suffered in the manner recorded of Jesus. There was, however, this difference. The Turin Shroud had not been wrapped round a body, as indicated by *John*, but draped lengthwise over it from the feet to the head, and then over the head, and so back to the feet, leaving the sides open. Clearly no such image (front and back) could appear if the wrappings had been round and round the body like a bandage. Was the Shroud genuine, and had John's Gospel been wrong?

This is not the place to deal with the issues in any detail, especially the origins of the relic. But the present writer has been in regular contact with the studies and scientific experiments of those seeking to determine whether the Shroud could indeed be the cloth which was in contact with the body of Jesus, and also participated in the British Conference devoted to the evidences. These, as may be imagined, have not proved conclusive either way.[4] But there are particular points relating to the image itself which are pertinent to the quest in which we are engaged. We are assuming hypothetically that the Shroud could be genuine.

One point that was made clear early on, long before systematic scientific studies, was that blood stains on the image suggested that the wounds had been bleeding after Jesus had been laid in the tomb, and that therefore he was still living at that time.

A second point is that the Shroud had not been used as a winding-sheet – if in fact it had been employed for the body of Jesus. It had merely been draped over him from feet to head, leaving both sides open. This does not look like the intentional burial of a man known to be dead. It looks much more like a temporary expedient, providing a clean protective covering without risk of suffocation pending arrangements for medical treatment elsewhere.

The circumstances could favour a plan to beat the authorities, and conceivably save the victim from death. This is quite different from the apologetic' explanatory proposition exclusive to *Matthew* (xxvii.62–66), that the Jewish authorities had anticipated an intention by the disciples of Jesus to abstract his dead body from the tomb in order to give verisimilitude to his claim that within three days he would rise from the dead. In fact *Matthew* is contradicted by *John*, who declares that he and Peter had not known that Jesus must rise from the dead until they found that his body was missing from the tomb (*Jn*.xx.8–9). Whatever had actually taken place, or been contrived, none of the scenarios lends credence to the claim that Jesus – in whatever manner brought back to life or restored to consciousness – was almost immediately able to engage in arduous travel.[5] The presumption is that in one manner or another his career in this world had ended.

### Chapter Seven

# Thomas Twin

The view that has been pressed most persistently in certain Muslim circles is that which has sought to identify the mysterious Yus–Asaph of Eastern tradition with what might be called the further adventures of Jesus Christ. To make that identification stick oriental records have been ransacked, and there has been resort to the most far-fetched interpretations. Those responsible, some of them of great learning and piety, must not be blamed too much, if at all. The Yus–Asaph of the legends is such a strange and outstanding personality, so much a figure from an alien environment and religion, that the only Jewish prophet of note who seemed to have some likeness to him was Jesus.

But, as we have established, such a conclusion – that Yus–Asaph was Jesus – is quite untenable when the evidences are investigated. Who then can Yus–Asaph have been? There was this tale of *Barlaam and Joasaph* in its eastern form. Had there been a Joasaph (Yus–Asaph) on whom the tale was founded? Or had a work of fiction – partly based on the life of the Buddha – become historicised? In the West we know what happened with the fictitious Sherlock Holmes, whose personality was partly borrowed from real life. When we look at the external evidences relating to Yus–Asaph, and notably those connected with his alleged tomb at Srinagar, we are impressed by the seeming dependence on legends which have become historicised.[1] We must seek to pursue the matter further. In support of the proposition that Yus–Asaph was Jesus there have been offered certain Gnostic and off-beat Christian records. One source put forward is the *Acts of Thomas*, dating from around the third century A.D. This relates the experiences of the Apostle Judas Thomas in India. Judas is sold by the resurrected Jesus to a merchant from that country who has been authorised by King Gundaphorus to buy him a slave who is a skilled carpenter. The merchant's name is given as Abbanes. Judas is taken to India, the land he is intended to evangelise, and the king calls upon him to build him a palace. Judas accepts large sums for the construction, which he proceeds to distribute to the poor. The palace, of course, as we learn, is never intended to be on earth: it will be the monarch's ultimate reward in heaven after he accepts Jesus as his saviour.

The book makes the point that Judas is called Thomas, which means twin, as being the twin of Jesus. The story is told in the book of how Jesus appears to a bridegroom, who believes he is Judas, whom he knows, until Jesus explains that he is his brother. This is hardly a foundation for the thesis that Jesus travelled to India, despite the fact that King Gundaphorus is known to history as a ruler who lived in the first century A.D.

However, there is a connection between the *Acts of Thomas* and the matters with which we are concerned, and this appears to have gone unnoticed. In *Thomas* the merchant called Abbanes later becomes the disciple and companion of Judas Thomas (the twin of Jesus). Now Dr A.C. Burnel reported a tradition concerning the Bani Israel, that when they came to N.W. India they requested through their leader to be permitted to settle. The leader's name is given as Isappu Habban.[2] Here the saint and his disciple are treated as a single individual. Isappu represents Josasaph (Isa – Jesus – blended with Asaph), who is also Yus-Asaph, and Habban is of course Abbanes. The Arabic version of *Barlaam and Joasaph* gives the name Abbabid as that of the disciple who serves and accompanies the saint in his travels, and finally attends him at his death in Kashmir.[3] We also need to note that Abbener is the father of Joasaph in the Greek version of the book, and he eventually becomes a Christian.

We should also recall here the account of Yuz-Asaf and his travels set down by Shaikh Al-Said in the 10th century A.D. He too speaks of the death of the saint in Kashmir cared for by his disciple named Ba'bad.[4]

It becomes feasible that in the story of *Barlaam and Joasaph*, as it originated, two lines of tradition have been brought together. The one was linked with the life of the Buddha, while the other was related to the missionary journeys and final death of the Apostle Judas Thomas.

Let us for a while pursue the Judas Thomas tradition to discover what further help it may afford us. The somewhat Ebionite-Gnostic *Acts of Thomas* does not correspond with the Yus-Asaph story as regards the death of the hero. Judas Thomas suffers martyrdom in India by being pierced with lances. He is buried in a tomb on a mountain. But then it is said that, as in the case of Jesus, the sepulchre was found empty, "for one of the brethren had stolen him away and taken him into Mesopotamia."[5] Other records say that Judas died and was buried at a city of India called Calamina, a name I have not been able to identify.[6] Consistent with the conjunction of the Buddha-Judas material we have variants of Yus-Asaph as Budhasaf and Yudasaf. Thomas in many of the Syrian and Egyptian Gnostic sources has the name Judas (Judah), so that he is Judas Thomas (Judah the Twin), just as the chief of the Apostles is Simon Peter (Simon the Rock). The Wandering Judas, who travelled to the East, could conceivably have had something to do with the legend of the Wandering Jew (i.e. Judean).[7]

In Yus-Asaph, and variants, we are similarly presented with a double-named individual. The first name – according to the sources – could have derived, depending on what line of tradition was followed, from Buddha, Judas, or Joseph, though not Jesus which is Isa in Arabic. Asaph in Hebrew usually equates with Collector. Another Judas, Judas Maccabaeus, appears in Jewish records as Collector.[8]

There is a mystery about the name of the Messiah (Christ) as there is about the name of the True Teacher of the Essenes, which initially brought us into contact with the Joseph-Asaph association. In the *Acts of Thomas* King Misdaeus asks the Apostle for the name of his Master and Judas Thomas tells him, "Thou canst not hear his true name at this time; but the name that was given him is Jesus Christ."[9]

It is evident that in the Judas Thomas traditions we have another link with the Yus-Asaph stories. And since Judas is represented as the twin of Jesus this could have a bearing on how Yus-Asaph came to be identified with Jesus. We have shown how the one called Abbanes (Habban) appears both in *Barlaam and Joasaph* and the *Acts of Thomas*. The circumstances clearly call for further investigation.

According to Rendel Harris, who was an authority on the Eastern Churches, there is no justification for crediting that Judas Thomas did visit India, though his mission field was Parthia. The Syrian Churches of Southern India, as in Malabar, whose members were known as Christians of St. Thomas, were really created by the Nestorians, who spread the Thomas association eastward. Harris quotes G.M. Rae in confirmation. "The fact that this mission is also Persian is corroborated by the mixture of Old Persian inscriptions with Syriac in the South Indian Churches, which proves them to be Nestorian foundations."[10]

We may then be concerned not so much with the movements of particular individuals, as with the movements of ideas giving rise to legends about certain people.

There could be a missionary link between the Nestorians and the Bani Israel; for Musaeus, the Bishop of Aduli, found in the fourth century A.D. many churches and synagogues in N.W.India, and particularly in Sihind, and he learnt of the connection with the Bani Israel of the West Coast of India.[11] Through unorthodox Christian channels it was spread in the East first that Jesus and Judas had been twins; and then among those of other faiths it could be supposed that really they were aspects of one and the same person, two heads on one neck.

How the idea arose that Jesus and Judas were twins is traced by Rendel Harris to Edessa, which had been a seat of worship of the *Heavenly Twins* (the Dioscuri), there known as Aziz and Monim, the accessors of the Sun-god. He goes on to say:

There can be little doubt in the mind of anyone who examines carefully the Edessan *Acts of Thomas*, that the writer of those *Acts* regarded Jesus and Judas as a pair of Heavenly Twins or Dioscuri, that he ascribed to them a number of popular traits of the great Twin Brethren, and that he uses his romance in order to displace the existing worship of the Dioscuri in Edessa by the Christian Religion."[12]

However this may be – and the substitution of Christian for Pagan personalities was a well-known missionary practice with the Church – here is evidence enough that Jesus and Judas Thomas were brought together in Islamic tales. Thomas is with Jesus on his travels from the Holy Land to the East. This is reported in the *Rauza-tus-Safa* of Mir Muhammad, dating from 1417 A.D., but printed and published in Bombay in 1832. In the Islamic tales Jesus and his associates went from Syria to Nasibain (Nisibis). There he was persecuted by the king, and continued his eastward journey. The Nisibis referred to is held to be the one between Syria and Mosul in Iraq, and thus close to Urfa (Edessa).[13] It was after leaving Nisibis, according to this view, that Jesus took the name of Yuz-Asaf. We may have here an indirect allusion to the twinning of Jesus and Judas Thomas which began at Edessa, and which had its impact on the composition of the *Acts of Thomas* and of *Barlaam and Joasaph*.

On the alleged route Jesus (now Yuz-Asaf) is said to have paid a visit to the tomb of Shem son of Noah.[14] Now Shem was the source from whom the Essenes claimed much of their special knowledge, including that of medicine.[15] And with this knowledge there was latterly associated the name of Asaph son of Berechiah, a name which also reached the Far East.

In Iraq the name of Shem might be substituted readily for that of the Babylonian Sun-God Shamash. We would be in the climate of thought relating to King Solomon as Sun King, contemporary of Asaph ben Berechiah, and type of the Messiah, and to the Essene and early Christian greeting of the rising sun.

The author of *Jesus in Heaven on Earth* usefully adds to our information from his own researches. He states (p.359): "In *Farhang-i-Jahangiri*, as in *Anjuman-i-Arae Nasiri*, we find Asaf was one of the grandees of non-Arab (*Ajami*) countries. In *Ghias-ul-Lughat* and *Burhan-Qate* Asaf is given as the name of a son of Barkhia, who was one of the learned of Bani Israel." He is puzzled, however, why Jesus should have assumed the name of Yuz-Asaf especially the Asaf part. He feels that he is helped to a solution by a book entitled *Farhang-i-Asafia*, where it is said: "In the time of Hazrat Isa (Jesus) when lepers were cured by him, they, on being admitted among healthy people, who were free from all disease, were called *Asaf*" (vol.*I*, 91). He concludes that Yuz-Asaf meant something like "Leader of Cured Lepers."

This is an interesting suggestion, though it proves to be a misleading one. The *Asaf*, in the significance of cured lepers, can be traced to the Egyptian priest, Manetho's, account of the Exodus of the Israelites from Egypt. This was quoted by Josephus in his tract against Apion.[16] The story went that an Egyptian Pharaoh, Amenophis, desiring to behold the gods, was told by a priest that this would be granted to him if he cleansed Egypt of all lepers and unclean persons. This was done, and these people were sent to the eastern quarries to the number of 80,000. They founded the city of Avaris, and settled there under the leadership of one called Osarsiph, and later joined forces with the Hyksos of Jerusalem against the Egyptians.

Here we have an old antisemitic tale that was going around in the Near East in the time of Jesus. In my reference to it elsewhere I had pointed out: "In this story there is a fusion of Joseph and Moses.[17] The leader of the outcasts is called Osarsiph by Egyptianising the name Joseph. The Jo (Greek Io) has been taken to represent the Hebrew God-name, and for this the Egyptian Osar (Osiris) has been substituted." I further described how the story became linked with

Jesus. I had not been aware at the time how, in the strange way of legends, Osarsiph would acquire a connection with Yus-Asaph.

The translators of the Greek *Barlaam and Joasaph* (*Loeb Classical Library*) took the Jo or Io of the name Joasaph to represent the Greek form of the Hebrew Yahweh (Yah), and interpret the name in a footnote as "The Lord gathers". They do not explain, however, why an Indian monarch should give his son a Hebrew name, or why it should be this one. Of course in the Eastern traditions Yus-Asaph is a Jew, and a Jew with a disguised name, going back ultimately, as we have proposed, to the Biblical antetypes of Joseph and Asaph in respect of the True Teacher. In Arabic the Yus part of the conjoined name would certainly appear to be a contraction of Joseph (Yusuf), just as the variants Yud and Bud can be held to have a connection with Judah and the Buddha.

But lurking in the background of the *Joasaph* story, as we need to remind ourselves, is also the name of Barachias, who eventually succeeded Joasaph as king. This makes it evident that the Asaph son of Berechiah tradition is involved, which has cropped up so curiously and surprisingly in Eastern folklore. It was evidently known at least to Arabic-speaking people that the name Asaf had the significance it bears in Hebrew of Gatherer or Collector. Judas Maccabaeus had acted in that capacity in relation to the Sacred Books in the time of persecution when the True Teacher was around in the second century B.C.

It is very difficult, and perhaps impossible, to get completely out of the woods. We are presented with the founder figure behind the Essenes, their Prophet and Lawgiver, somehow through legends and traditions marching through history and travelling to the East as a mysterious white-robed Jewish prophet with an assumed name. Because of such books as the *Acts of Thomas* and *Barlaam and Joasaph*, and for other reasons, this personality became identified with Jesus. This last conclusion, at least, we may claim to have eliminated at this stage of our inquiry.

But what are we left with? The strong possibility, which cannot amount to a certainty, that the True Teacher, to escape his enemies travelled first from Syria to Mesopotamia, and then on to Kashmir, where in due course he died . In this case it may well be his tomb that has for centuries been venerated at Srinagar.

### Chapter Eight

# Refugees of Religion

In all the sources we have employed a fairly constant ingredient has been a movement eastward of refugees for religion's sake, whether as clans or as individuals. And this is associated with calamities and persecutions affecting the Jewish homeland. We have encountered it in the traditions of the Afghans and of the Bani Israel, and in the land of Kashmir. There came to be included in such traditions references to the Lost Ten Tribes of Israel, from the time when they had disappeared into the East. But it is evident from the sources we have examined that no recollections of the captivity of Israel in the eighth century B.C. are indicated. To all intents and purposes the Jews in the East became the legatees of *all* Israel.[1] Many Jews had remained in Babylonia from the captivity of Judah (the Southern Kingdom), and under the Persians their numbers were swollen by emigrants.

In the *Book of Esther* in the Bible we read how the Persian monarch Ahasuerus wrote both to the Persian authorities in the Provinces and to the Jewish representatives in them, "which are from India unto Ethiopia, an hundred and twenty and seven provinces," each according to their languages, including Hebrew (*Esther* viii). With the conquests of Alexander the Great a number of Jews reached India as members of his army. Some 250 years later the large communities of Jews in the East were swollen by refugees from Palestine fleeing from the Romans. Then there were the sectarian migrations from persecution by the Jewish Sadducees, and ultimately from the fourth century A.D. the Jewish sectarians and unorthodox Christians who fled from the persecutions of the Byzantine Church.

We should not expect from the later religious and sectarian literature any clear-cut descriptions of past events and experiences, or, still more, of beliefs. Dissenting and minority groups especially, which had good reason to be reticent in order to survive, and whose doctrines often tended towards the esoteric, did not favour being too explicit either in speech or in writing. Such bodies also were much more open to changes as a result of interpretations by later teachers and adjustments to new geographical environments. Their views and traditions were also not infrequently influenced by their being forced for self-preservation to adopt outwardly the dominant faith of the regions in which they were located.

A case in point is that of the mysterious Nusairiyeh of the Near East. Dr Thomson of *The Land and the Book* fame in Victorian times had several encounters with them. He reports that they were extremely evasive about their religion. They claimed to be Christians, though not like others, honouring Moses and Jesus. Persecution by the followers of Islam had made them very wary. Their ceremonies were held in secret, and the author reports that, "Should any of their number divulge their mysteries, he would be assassinated without remorse, mercy, or delay." These people would appear to have inherited some teachings from the Essenes.

It has been abundantly evident with the sources utilised in our quest that we cannot take things at face value, though the information given is frequently of service. We have to recognise the part played by a variety of factors in blending doctrines and transmitting traditions. Often those sects of later times had no clear understanding of where their founding fathers had stood, and what had been their experiences. Certain things had been handed down, but in so garbled and confused a manner that often it is extremely difficult – and sometimes impossible – to extract reliable information, especially about persons and events of ancient times.

An important and relevant example is that of the Mandaeans of the Lower Euphrates, who at one time were well-represented in the proximity of Basra and Kut in Iraq. By the Arabs they are known as Subbas (Baptists), and by the Jesuit missionaries of the 17th century they were called Christians of St. John (i.e. the Baptist). Their own literature will have it that they are Nazoreans, and the hero of their faith is the Messianic figure of John the son of Zechariah.

These people have a kinship in origin and experiences with other Nazoreans, who were the Jewish adherents of Jesus as Messiah. The name has no connection with the town of Nazareth, and signifies Guardians or Custodians (of certain information or teaching). In the present century a great deal of their surviving literature has become accessible through the efforts of scholars like Lidzbarski and Lady Drower. The latter devoted many years to Mandaean studies, and on the spot researches. Unfortunately very little of this material is known to the general public, or even to many students of religion.

In Mandaean teaching John the Baptist is greater than Jesus. He is the Man from Above planted in the womb of his elderly mother Elizabeth, and he also partly reflects aspects of the Babylonian god Oannes, who, according to legend, landed in the Persian Gulf. Thus John is the true 'fisher of men' and also the 'good shepherd'. In various respects he has taken on the colouring of his Babylonian environment.

But the Mandaean–Nazoreans have retained some recollection of their historical origins and experiences. They claim that their ancestors were the victims of a persecution in Judaea, which can be dated in 37 A.D.[3]

In previous studies of mine I have suggested that this persecution could be the same as that which involved the Nazorean followers of the Way, and was conducted by Saul of Tarsus (afterwards the Apostle Paul) according to Christian tradition.[4] As already mentioned the Judaeo–Christian *Clementine Recognitions* also refers to this event, and speaks of 5,000 of the brethren arriving first of all at Jericho, and evidently continuing to a place of asylum in the Land of Damascus.[5] Here they would be received by the Essenes of those parts, of whom Ananias of Damascus mentioned in the *Acts of the Apostles* (ix. 10–17) was a representative. Saul himself, after his conversion, may well have stayed with one of the communities during the two years that he was in 'Arabia'. There are a number of reflections of Essene teaching in his available letters as Paul the Apostle.

From the Hauran the ancestors of the Mandaean–Nazoreans in due course moved on via Haran to northern Iraq, and finally to the region of the Persian Gulf.

The experiences of these people, their flight and migrations – largely along the route taken by other bodies with which they had some spiritual affinity – their somewhat garbled traditions, which yet contain folk memories of historical worth, are thus typical of the circumstances which confront us in the quest we have been pursuing.

Geographical and political references are of particular worth where they do not serve any propagandist intention. And as it happens those that concern us have much in common, where they provide links between the Holy Land and Mesopotamia, and second the northern and southern routes to India.

With the first we follow the so-called Fertile Crescent, the road travelled westward by Abraham from Ur of the Chaldees to Canaan. There was ample scope over a great stretch of the way for groups of dissidents and sectarians to find refuge in tolerable but not too hospitable zones. Some, like the Essenes and then the Christian-Nazoreans had been content to remain on the fringe of the western end of the arc. They were not strongly missionary bodies: they were seeking to live in loyal commitment to the Divine behests while waiting for the End Time circumstances which would enable them to return to their homeland and participate in the felicities of the Messianic Age. But also, naturally, they gave a welcome, as we have illustrated, to later emigrants who also were seeking asylum to preserve their faith.

The first substantial trek to the Land of Damascus had taken place in the time of the True Teacher in the second century B.C.[6] He had pledged his followers to the observance of the New Covenant. We may take it from the *Damascus Document* that the communities of the Saints continued in exile for several generations, though some individuals fell away. Inspired by the conviction that the Last Times had arrived, a move was made towards the close of the first century B.C. to stage a partial return and reactivate an old centre near the Dead Sea. But those who reposed Messianic hopes in John the Baptist and Jesus found themselves affected by the fate which overtook them.

There came another persecution, in which Saul of Tarsus was active. As a result of this some thousands of adherents fled across the Jordan near Jericho, and travelled north through Peraea to the Hauran where they were given asylum. But there was a greater flight from Judaea thirty years later at the beginning of the Jewish Revolt against Rome. The Dead Sea centre at Qumran was abandoned. Multitudes of the Jewish followers of Jesus, with members of his family, travelled to what had now become a homeland for those of the Way. Three hundred years later, as Epiphanius records, their communities were to be found scattered over a wide area along the fringe of the route from Palestine to Mesopotamia, some having grown more eccentric or ascetic, but still preserving memories of their origins and producing literature of their tenets. A proportion, and not an inconsiderable one, in course of time moved on still further to the east and south-east.

But we have to think not only of community migrations, but of beliefs and literature carried along the trade routes. In many cases those who conveyed them were Jewish merchants, like those who had been instrumental in converting the rulers of Adiabene to Judaism in the first century A.D. The royal house of Adiabene

supported the messianically influenced Jewish Revolt against the
Romans in A.D.67-70, in which the Temple at Jerusalem perished. So
it is of concern to our theme that Dr A. Mingana should have stated:[7]

The nerve-centre of this movement towards Christian beliefs in Central
Asia, and even in India, was undoubtedly the province of Adiabene situated
East of the Tigris, between two of its historic tributaries: the Greater and the
Lesser Zabs. The capital of this province was Arbel, the numerous Jewish
population of which was so much in the ascendant at the beginning of the
Christian era . . . Even as far West as the right bank of the Tigris, near the
modern town of Mosul, the Jews had erected a fortress called *hisna 'ebraya*
'The Hebrew Fort,' which existed down to the Arab invasion.

While the quest for areas in the East where sectarians could practise
their religion with less fear of persecution continued, there was now,
with the spread of Christianity, an intensification of missionary zeal.
Prominent in the East in this respect were the Nestorians, themselves
at odds with the Orthodox Church. Curiously for our theme one of
their number in the sixth century A.D. was Joseph a physician, who
became Patriarch of the Nestorians in 552. Some two hundred years
later another Nestorian, the Patriarch Timothy, was particularly
active in inspiring evangelical activity. He speaks of this in one of his
letters, relating that in his time "many monks crossed the sea and
went to the Indians and the Chinese with only a rod and a scrip."[8]

Mingana quotes a letter to the Patriarch from 'Abdisho, the
Metropolitan of Merw, where it is related:[9]

A king from the Turkish kings became Christian with two hundred
thousand souls. The cause of this was that he lost his way when he went
hunting, and while he was bewildered, not knowing what to do, he saw the
figure of a man who promised salvation to him. He asked him for his name,
and he told him it was Mar Sergius. He intimated to him to become
Christian, and said to him, 'close your eyes', and he closed them. When he
opened them, he found himself in his camp. He was amazed at this, and he
made inquiries concerning the Christian religion . . .

The travels to the Far East of individual missionary monks, and
the encounter with one of them just quoted, remind us of the story of
how around 75 A.D. the Rajah Shalewahin met a mysterious
personality from the West robed in white, who called himself
Yusashaphat, and who declared his function to be that of purifying
religion.[10]

It rather looks as if in course of time the escapes to the East of
various refugee Jewish sectarians and others in the first and second
century A.D. became confused with those of others, mainly unorthodox Christians, who acted as missionaries in subsequent centuries.

Especially in the region of Western Afghanistan, which became a meeting place of Buddhism, Judaism, Christianity and Islam, not to mention elements of Zoroastrianism, all kinds of combinations seem to have resulted.

In the region of Herat in modern times O.M. Burke encountered the remnants of such a fusion in a nominally Muslim sect claiming to be followers of Jesus, identified with Yuz-Asaf the Kashmiri. They were in possession of a holy book quite distinct from the Gospels and entitled *Traditions of the Messiah*. Unfortunately, Burke does not relate the contents of this book. But in what he reports of the sect's teaching there was a mixture of elements from various religions, including relics of Essene and Nazorean concepts.[11]

Burke's experience well illustrates the persistence of traditions and beliefs through many centuries, and how they could be combined and adapted, so that early and late materials were confused and alien features introduced, and even given distinctive slants.

What is significant, and most impressive in relation to our investigation, is the tenacity of distinctively Essene positions and traditions centuries after the Essenes, as a distinct and independent body, had ceased to be operative. Somehow the True Teacher in his Joseph-Asaph guise lived on, and what he had represented endured, even though few if any could tell about him as a person, and his image was confused with those of other great religious figures.

### Chapter Nine

# The Son of Man

The pursuit in which we have been engaged has led us to many strange places, often remote from one another in time and space. In widespread legends and traditions we have been able to detect likenesses and associations which seem to reflect the transmission of ideas which have had an appeal – albeit in very different contexts and surroundings. They suggest a common origin; but one that remains in the background, undisclosed and almost entirely unrecognised. This was because those who reported the circumstances had not turned in the right direction, and indeed were largely unacquainted with it. It was the discovery of the Dead Sea Scrolls that, if we were open-minded, could begin to put us on the right track.

The most instructive outcome of our quest has been the revelation that underlying the phenomena we have encountered is an ideology emanating substantially from those mysterious Hebrew philosophers of history, the Essenes. And more than this, it focuses upon the experiences of an exceptional man, discovered to us as the True Teacher, or Teacher of Righteousness. This man, Prophet, Priest and Lawgiver, was to be magnified into the Messianic Son of Man, the exalted expression of our common humanity, nameless and timeless; and also to be manifest among us as the lowly and lonely bearer of our sufferings and victim of our inhumanity. The Hebraism, Son of Man, simply means a member of the human race – Man as conceived by God. About his lowly – that is to say earthly – manifestation, it was held by the Teacher's followers that the pseudonyms and antetypes of Joseph and Asaph had significant things to reveal. But fundamentally he is the reflection of God in creation, who ultimately in miniature manifestation will come into his own on our minute selected planet.

Here we make contact with the inner secret of the Essene legacy as represented by the True Teacher. He comes among us not once, but from time to time as may be essential; occasionally – though rarely – in the white garment of his priestly calling, the Jew who is also

Everyman. No one knows his real name, or can describe his face, or tell positively anything about him.

He is the ideal of our species incognito. He may be encountered in East and West, in the past, in the present, and in the future, by any of us of any faith and clime. He is the immortal traveller, who has endured all the adversities our planet can inflict. Wherever he is found he calls us back to our better selves, to the path of concern for others, to love and goodness of heart. He restores our courage and our hope.

He is eternally adaptable, so that in all our diversities we are at home with him, and he is our home. He is also the goal towards which we strive, the World Man of a wiser, nobler world we visualise in our finer imaginations. Through him, in spirit, we reach out to wonders infinite and glories incomparable.

Perhaps the Essenes did not fully appreciate what they were communicating to us when they set out the Son of Man doctrine. We have some of their literature, and some reflections of their visions in other literature. But even with the discovery of the Dead Sea Scrolls we have not broken through completely to the core of their vision, and how it should be interpreted. We do have, however, relics of how it was depicted and how it was taken up by those who saw in the Messianic figures of John the Baptist, and more strikingly Jesus, the True Teacher of the Last Times, the Son of Man incarnate. Indeed it would appear that Jesus specifically identified himself with the ful-filment of the Essene Hope. I have to some extent dealt with this theme in previous books of mine;[1] but it is pertinent, and indeed essential, to go over the ground again – especially as regards source material – since its implications have largely not been grasped or for credal reasons have been set on one side.

We begin with two fragments of the Essene *Commentary on Psalm xxxvii*. On verses 23-24: 'The steps of the Man are confirmed by the Lord and He delights in all his ways; though (he stumble, he shall not fall, for the Lord shall support his hand). Interpreted, this concerns the Priest the Teacher of (Righteousness . . . whom) He established to build for Himself the congregation of . . ." Here it is clear that the Essenes identified the mysterious Man of their doctrine with the True Teacher. On verses 32-33: "The wicked watches out for the righteous and seeks (to slay him. The Lord will not abandon him into his hand or) let him be condemned when he is tried. Interpreted, this concerns the Wicked (Priest) who (rose up against the Teacher of

Righteousness] that he might put him to death [because he served the truth] and the Law, [for which reason] he (i.e. the Wicked Priest) laid hands upon him. But God will not abandon [him into his hand, and will not let him be condemned when he is tried. And [God] will pay him (i.e. the Wicked Priest) his reward by delivering him into the hand of the violent of the nations, that they may execute upon him [the judgements of wickedness]."[2]

But was the Man only the True Teacher? On this Dr Vermes, whose rendering of the Dead Sea Scrolls we have given here, has this to say. "If I have understood it correctly the functions ascribed to the person alluded to in the Community Rule (IV) as *geber* (i.e. the Man) was to 'instruct the upright in the knowledge of the Most High' at the end of time, and 'to teach the wisdom of the Sons of Heaven to the perfect of way'... Are we justified in concluding that the Prophet, or *geber*, and the Teacher of Righteousness are all one and the same person? If so, it would seem to lead to the hypothesis that after a certain moment in its history all mention of the expected Prophet, or *geber*, vanished from the sect's writings because it had come to believe that he had already appeared in the person of the Teacher of Righteousness."[3]

This view has some justification, but it does not go far enough. For the Essenes the True Teacher clearly was the Man, but we must preferably describe him as the Man incarnate, the earthly manifestation of the Sky Man in whose likeness Adam was created.

The mystery of Sky Man was one of the great secrets studied by the Essenes and other Jewish mystics. He is referred to as the Man, or Son of Man, the *Adam Kadmon* (Archetypal Man), and his incarnation will reverse the consequences of the human Adam's sin, and restore the Rule of God on earth. In the Essene *Community Rule (IV)* it is said:

In the mysteries of His understanding, and in His glorious wisdom, God has ordained an end for falsehood, and at the Time of the Visitation He will destroy it for ever. Then Truth, which has wallowed in the ways of wickedness during the dominion of falsehood until the appointed Time of Judgement, shall arise in the world for ever. God will then purify every deed of Man with His truth; He will refine for Himself the human frame by rooting out all spirit of falsehood from the bounds of his flesh. He will cleanse him of all wicked deeds with the spirit of holiness; like purifying waters He will shed upon him the spirit of truth (to cleanse) him of all abomination and false-hood. And he shall be plunged into the spirit of purification that he may instruct the upright in the knowledge of the Most High, and teach the

wisdom of the Sons of Heaven to the perfect of way. For God has chosen them
for an everlasting Covenant and all the glory of Adam shall be theirs. There
shall be no more lies and all the works of falsehood shall be put to shame.

Thus ultimately human society will be redeemed. "All the glory
of Adam shall be theirs." But the process comes in stages. First Sky
Man, who is the image of God, must be incarnated on earth in the
True Teacher. Then the Teacher, who sets the example and is persecuted by the forces of evil, wins a following – the pious in Israel –
who share His tribulations, and thus qualify as the Son of Man
collective, as in the vision of Daniel (*Dan*.vii. 15-28). A description of
Sky Man in all his awesome majesty, clad in pure linen like a priestly
Essene, is furnished in *Daniel* x.4-7.[5]

When the Redemption did not speedily come as anticipated this
did not destroy the faith of the faithful. The Last Times were now
calculated to arrive around the period corresponding to the latter
part of the first century B.C., when the True Teacher of the Last
Times would manifest himself, fulfilling the functions of the earlier
nameless Teacher, and having transferred to him the incarnation of
Sky Man. We have to appreciate that over a period of about a century
and a half there had been a reassessment of the interpretations of the
Essene texts with their pseudonymous allusions. And they would
come to be further adapted by those who claimed for John the
Baptist and for Jesus the rôle of the True Teacher who incarnated Sky
Man, as we shall illustrate.

In its more developed form we have an elaboration of the Son of
Man doctrine in the *Similitudes of Enoch*, which is possibly early
Judaeo–Christian and follows Essene concepts. In vision Enoch finds
himself in the Heavenly Courts, and there beholds the Son of Man.

And there I saw One who had a Head of Days (i.e.*Daniel's* Ancient of Days),
and His head was white like wool, and with Him was another being whose
countenance had the appearance of a man whose face was full of gracious-
ness, like one of the holy angels. And I asked the angel, who went with me
and showed me all the hidden things, concerning that Son of Man, who he
was, and whence he was, and why he went with the Head of Days. And he
answered and said unto me, 'This is the Son of Man who hath righteousness,
with whom dwelleth righteousness, and who reveals all the treasures of that
which is hidden, because the Lord of Spirits hath chosen him, and his lot
before the Lord of Spirits hath surpassed everything in uprightness for ever.
And this Son of Man whom thou hast seen . . . will put down the kings from
their thrones and kingdoms because they do not extol and praise Him (i.e.
the Lord of Spirits), nor thankfully acknowledge whence the kingdom was
bestowed upon them . . .'

And at that hour that Son of Man was named in the presence of the Lord of Spirits and his name before the Head of Days. And before the sun and the signs were created, before the stars of heaven were made, his name was named before the Lord of Spirits. He will be a staff to the righteous on which they will support themselves and not fall, and he will be the light of the Gentiles and the hope of those who are troubled in heart. And all who dwell on earth will fall down and bow the knee before him, and bless and laud and celebrate with song the Lord of Spirits. And for this cause has he been chosen and hidden before him before the creation of the world and for evermore. And the wisdom of the Lord of Spirits hath revealed him to the holy and righteous, because they have hated and despised this world of unrighteousness . . .' And in those days the kings of the earth, and the strong who possess the earth, will be of downcast countenance . . . And I will give them over into the hands of Mine Elect Ones . . . Before them they will fall and not rise again . . . for they have denied the Lord of Spirits and His anointed.

And the Lord of Spirits seated him (the Son of Man) on the throne of his glory, and the spirit of righteousness was poured out upon him, and the word of his mouth slew all the sinners . . . And all the Elect will stand before him in that day . . . And the righteous and the Elect will be saved on that day and will never again from thenceforth see the faces of the sinners and unrighteous. And the Lord of Spirits will abide with them for ever, and with that Son of Man will they eat and lie down and rise up for ever.[6]

There is an echo here of a number of passages in the Gospels where Jesus is speaking of the Son of Man, and we come close to Pauline Christology relating to the Second Adam and to the predestination of the Elect.[7] And here we mark what appears to be the ultimate fusion of the Messianic Hope relating to the Priestly and Davidic Messiahs. In the Son of Man concept christology and eschatology meet.

A foreshadowing of this can be seen in the Essene psalms, where we read:

> "For the children have come to the throes of death,
>     and she labours in her pains who bears the Man.
> For amid the throes of death
>     she shall bring forth a Man-child,
> and amid the pains of hell
>     there shall spring from her child-bearing crucible
>     a Marvellous Mighty Counsellor;[8]
> and the Man shall be delivered from out the throes."[9]

In the New Testament the *Revelation* (xii. 1-6) puts the birth of the Man in its cosmic context; and it is clear from the birth stories of John the Baptist as the Priestly Messiah and of Jesus as the Davidic Messiah that the cosmic situation is tranferred to the plane of history. When the time comes for the earthly birth of the Man there is an attempt by the threatened Forces of Evil to compass his destruction. "The Dragon stood before the woman which was ready to be delivered, for to devour her child as soon as it was born" (*Rev*.xii.4). In the terrestrial birth stories, in the case of Jesus, the infant Messiah is taken to Egypt to escape the sword of Herod, while in the case of John the Baptist his mother, for the same reason, flies with him into the wilderness.[10]

The Essene tradition clarifies for us the significance of these birth stories by claiming that the True Teacher had been an incarnation of the Heavenly Man. Both John and Jesus were seen as the True Teacher of the Last Times, and consequently for their followers they also were incarnations of Sky Man (the Son of Man). This was initially understood of Jesus by his Jewish followers, but the teaching became perverted by the Christian Church in its development and resulted in the doctrine of the Trinity.

From Mandaean-Nazorean sources we are given information about the incarnation of Sky Man (called the Light-Adam) in John the Baptist. And since this information will not be known to many we will cite passages from the Mandaean *Book of John*[11] (section 18).

In vision there is seen the appearance of a star which stands over Enishbai (i.e. Elizabeth) while fire burns in Old Father Zakhria. Word is sent to Lilyukh (i.e. Elijah, in Hebrew *Elijahu*) so that he may explain the vision. This he does in the following terms: "The star, that came and stood over Enishbai: a child will be planted out of the height from Above. He comes and will be given to Enishbai. The fire, that burned in Old Father Zakhria: Yohana will be born in Jerusalem." When the news is broken to Zechariah he is incredulous, and exclaims, "Where is there a dead man who becomes living again, that Enishbai should bear a child? . . . It is two and twenty years today that I have seen no wife. Nay, neither through me nor through you will Enishbai bear a child." He is advised, however, that "the child shall be planted from out of the Most High Height, and be given to thee in thy old age." The child is duly planted in the womb of Elizabeth and John is born. After his birth, however, he was mysteriously conveyed to Parwan, the white mountain, and his parents did not see him again until he was 22, when he was brought on a cloud of splendour and set down in the region of Jerusalem, there to be reunited with his mother and Zechariah.

John is referred to here as "the youth, the Man, who is sent by the King (i.e. God)."

The Mandaean story has become legendary in the course of time, but retains significant traces of the initial version of the Messianic birth of John the Baptist. Something is owed to Babylonian religion with its representation of the airborne God-Man, as with Daniel's Son of Man who travels by cloud (*Dan*.vii.13); and inevitably Jesus as Son of Man is taken up to heaven and will return to earth on a cloud (*Lk*.xx.51; *Rev*.i.7). Appropriately, in the birth stories of John and Jesus in *Luke*, it is the angel Gabriel who is the instrument of revelation of their advents; for it is *Geber* (the Heavenly Man) who is to be incarnated.

In another context the Essene vision was passed on in the *Sibylline Oracles* venerated by the Romans, and interpolated by Jewish and Christian propagandists.[12] So we read: "And then shall God send from heaven a king, and shall judge every man in blood and blazing fire" (Bk.iii.286-287). And again: "And then shall God send from the sun a king,[13] who shall make all the earth cease from ruinous war, killing some, and with some making a sure agreement" (652-654).

Coinciding with the period when the Essenes awaited the manifestation of the True Teacher of the Last Times, in the second half of the first century B.C., we have the Roman author Virgil picking up the predictions as communicated by the Sybil of Cumae, foretelling the imminent Golden Age:

Now is come the Last Age of the song of Cumae; the great lines of the centuries begin anew. Now the Virgin returns, the reign of Saturn returns; now a new generation descends from heaven on high. Only do thou, pure Lucina, smile on the birth of the child, under whom the iron brood shall first cease, and a golden race spring up throughout the world! Thine own Apollo now is king!"[14]

## Chapter Ten

# The Essene Legacy

Early in the first century A.D. an offshoot of the Essenes flourished in Egypt under the Greek name of Therapeuts, and attracted the interest and approbation of the Jewish philosopher Philo of Alexandria. It is significant that among the manuscripts of the Essenes discovered by chance at the beginning of the ninth century were books of 'the Alexandrian', who no doubt was Philo. There is a clear kinship between the Essene concept of 'the Man' and Philo's eagerness to give a Jewish interpretation of the Platonic idea of the Logos.

Speaking of the Creation, Philo tells us that Light was an image of the Divine Word. It was an "Invisible Light perceptible only by Mind." From that "all-brightness" the sun, moon, stars and planets, drew portions according to their capacity; but the very process of change from invisible light to visible light inevitably involved a diminution of light's purity, because it was dimmed by entering the sphere of the senses.[1] Similarly Philo tells us that when man was made in the image of God this did not imply bodily form in God. It was man's mind which reflected the Mind of the universe as its archtetype.[2]

Those who live in the knowledge of the One are rightly called Sons of God (*Deut*.xiv.1.). "But if there be any as yet unfit to be called a Son of God, let him press to take his place under God's Firstborn, the Word, who holds the eldership among the angels, their ruler as it were. And many names are his, for he is called the Beginning (*arche*), and the Name of God, and His Word (*logos*), and the Man after His image . . . For if we have not yet become fit to be thought sons of God yet we may be sons of His invisible image, the most holy Word. For the Word is the eldest-born image of God."[3] In this respect "we are all sons of one Man" (*Gen*.xlii.11).

Other Philonic descriptions of the Logos reach us again through Christian channels.[4] The Word is High Priest of God, without sin, shadowed forth by Melchizedek. He is "an Advocate to obtain both forgiveness of sins and a supply of all good." The Word is the image (*eikon*) of God, by whom the whole universe was fashioned.

Elsewhere Philo elaborates the idea of the High Priest as representative of the Logos.

We say, then, that the High Priest is not a man, but a Divine Word and immune from all unrighteousness whether intentional or unintentional. For Moses says that he cannot defile himself (*Lev*.xxi. 11) either for the father (the mind), or for the mother (sense-perception), because methinks, he is the child of parents incorruptible and wholly free from stain, his father being God, who is likewise Father of all, and his mother Wisdom, through whom the universe came into existence; because moreover, his head has been anointed with oil, and by this I mean that his ruling faculty is illumined with a brilliant light, in such wise that he is deemed worthy 'to put on the garments' (i.e. of the high priesthood). Now the garments which the supreme Word of Him-that-is puts on as raiment are the World, for He arrays Himself in earth and air and water and fire and all that comes from these.[5]

The Philonic doctrine is linked with the Essene teaching concerning the Priestly Messiah (i.e. his head is anointed with oil), who finds his embodiment in the True Teacher, or Teacher of Righteousness. His antetype is seen in Melchizedek (whose name signifies True King or King of Righteousness), who is "priest of the Most High God" (*Gen*.xiv.18).[6] The conjunction of the Ruler of Israel with Melchizedek is made already in *Psalm* cx, a fact that influenced the Maccabaean Priest-kings from the time of John Hyrcanus I.

We turn here from Philo to the occult teaching of the Pharisees and later Rabbis. Their Secret Doctrines were felt to be so mentally and spiritually dangerous for the majority that it was laid down in the *Mishnah* (dating from the 2nd century A.D.):

Men are not to expound unlawful unions with a company of three, nor the *Lore of Creation* with two persons, nor the (Heavenly) *Chariot* (i.e. in *Ezekiel*) with one; but if a man do so, he must be a wise man, and one who has much knowledge on his own account. Everyone who meddles with these four things that follow, it were better for him if he had not come into the world: they are, What is Above and What is Below, What is Before and What is After. And everyone who does not revere the glory of his Maker (i.e. detracts from God's Unity and Incorporeality), it were better for him if he had not come into the world."[7]

It was in the *Lore of Creation* (*Maaseh Bereshith*) that Sky Man was represented, to convey how the visible universe proceeded from the invisible. The visible was not God, but the expression of His Attributes. The theme was developed in the *Sefer Yetsirah* (*Book of Creation*), where we encounter the Ten *Sefiroth*, the Divine attributes, with which were associated the 22 letters of the Hebrew alphabet. As Gershom Sholem has expressed it: "These together represent the mysterious forces whose convergence has produced the various combinations observable throughout the whole of creation; they are the 'thirty-two (10 |22) secret paths of wisdom', through which God has created all that exists."[8]

In one aspect the *Sefiroth* are represented as the Tree of Being, but more particularly as the *Adam Kadmon*, the Primordial Man, Sky Man, in whose image Adam was created. His head is a triad, Wisdom and Intelligence surmounted by the Crown representing Sovereignty. The breast which is Beauty is associated in the second triad with the right arm which is Mercy and the left arm which is Justice. In a third triad the genitalia which are Foundation govern the right leg which is Firmness and the left leg which is Splendour, which in turn make a triad with the feet which signify Kingdom.[9]

The visible universe, as a whole, thus has a Messianic significance and intention, made explicit on earth by the creation of Adam and the dominion entrusted to him. For this reason, for the redemption of mankind, Sky Man (the Man) could incarnate in the True Teacher, as believed by the followers of Jesus and of John the Baptist.

We shall be presenting the Early Christian philosophy, deriving from the Essenes, in the next chapter. Part of this interpretation drew also upon the opinions of Philo. But we may briefly anticipate here, by reference to the position taken up by the Ebionites, those Judaeo-Christians who were closest to the position of the Essenes.

According to the Ebionites: "Jesus was begotten of the seed of man, and was chosen; and so by that choice he was called Son of God from the Messiah that entered into him from above in the likeness of a dove. And they deny that he (i.e. Messiah) was begotten of God the Father, but say that he was created like one of the archangels, yet greater, and that he is lord of angels and of all things made by the Almighty . . . Messiah (as distinct from Jesus), they say, is a Manlike Figure, invisible to men in general.[10]

The alternative view about John the Baptist and Jesus was, as we have seen, that the incarnation of Sky Man (the Light Adam) in them took place in the wombs of their mothers. His Messianic nature, brought out in the *Similitudes of Enoch*,[11] as Master of Destiny in the fulfilment of God's plan in Creation, is represented by the Crown on the head of *Adam Kadmon*, and Kingdom which is beneath his feet.

The Rabbis who delved into the esoteric matters of the *Lore of*

*Creation* inevitably conceived the Archetypal Man as a vast universe-filling figure. And even the microcosm, the first man Adam upon earth, was held in his innocent state to have been of gigantic stature.

R.Eleazar said, The first man extended from the earth to the firmament, for it is said (*Deut*.iv.32), 'from the day that God created man *upon* the earth'. But in as much as he sinned, the Holy One – blessed be He – placed His hand upon him and made him small, as it is said (*Ps*.cxxxix.5), 'Thou hast fashioned me after and before, and laid Thine hand upon me' (i.e. two fashionings, one before Adam sinned and one afterwards). R.Jehudah said that Rab said, The first man extended from one end of the world to the other, for it is said, 'since the day that God created man upon the earth, and from one end of heaven to the other.' But in as much as he sinned, the Holy One – blessed be He – placed His hand upon him and made him small, as it is said, 'and laid Thine hand upon me.'[12]

It was also adduced that Adam in his sinless state was a being of transparent light, and only after his Fall from grace did he become opaque and skin-covered. In a manuscript of the Pentateuch in the possession of R.Meir (2nd century A.D.) the text in *Gen*.iii.7 read "coats of light" instead of "coats of skin." Thus initially Adam corresponded more nearly to his cosmic archetype. The text read by R.Meir was possibly an Essene copy in which the variant reading had been introduced deliberately. Biblical books among the Dead Sea Scrolls exhibit such variants made for didactic purposes. In one of the Gnostic systems described by the Church Father Irenaeus later in the same century it was said that before the Fall Adam and Eve had spiritual bodies like the angels, but afterwards their bodies grew dense and torpid and became "coats of skin".

Perhaps also dating from the late second century was a book which was favoured later by the Manichaeans, in which we have a Christianised form of this teaching. This was the *Acts of John* (in this case John son of Zebedee). Having referred to the transfiguration of Jesus, John continues:

And at another time he (Jesus) taketh with him me (John) and James and Peter into the mountain where he was wont to pray, and we saw in him a light such as it is not possible for a man who useth corruptible (mortal) speech to describe what it was like. Again in like manner he bringeth us three up into the mountain, saying, 'Come ye with me.' And we went again: and we saw him at a distance praying. I, therefore, because he loved me, drew nigh unto him softly, as though he could not see me, and stood looking at his hinder parts: and I saw that he was not in any wise clad with garments, but was seen of us naked, and not in any wise as a man, and that his feet were whiter than any snow, so that the earth was lighted up by his feet, and that his head touched the heaven; so that I was afraid and cried out, and he, turning about, appeared as a man of small stature, and caught hold on my beard and pulled it and said to me: 'John, be not faithless but believing, and not curious.'[13]

The account of the transfiguration, as we find it in the Gospels, is here expanded to emphasise the composite personality of Jesus in the capacity of Messiah, not as God and man, but as Archetypal Man and earthly man. This was something the majority of the Christian theologians who were converts from paganism did not apprehend, and accordingly they misunderstood and misinterpreted the New Testament records. The Church of today, still labouring under the credal follies of its Councils from the fourth century onwards, has not got round to making the theological adjustments which are called for. Indeed, there is no provision for such correction in theological studies, and the ordinary Bible reader is denied the explanatory notes and comments which would introduce him to the Essene and Jewish interpretations.

When we are given access to the legacy of the Essenes we are able to appreciate what they were seeking to transmit. It was for the high purpose of redeeming the Elect and finally the Earth itself, and incorporating the faithful in the Messianic personality, that the Heavenly Man, in whose image Adam had been created, had incarnated in the True Teacher in the End Time. This was the revelation given to the Jewish mystics, who accordingly, in moments of ecstacy, saw the earthly Son of Man in vast dimensions, symbolic of the universal proportions of Sky Man, and knew themselves to be comprehended in that Son of Man (*Dan.*vii.13-18,18).

### Chapter Eleven

# The Christian Heritage

When we now turn directly to the New Testament it becomes evident in the light of what we have adduced that what is asserted of Jesus is to be understood in relation to the Essene and esoteric Jewish concepts of that time. What is set down is the application of such teaching, as conceived by individual writers and not a substitute for it. Indeed, much of the Essene literature was regarded by the early Christians as divinely inspired, as for example in the *Epistle of Jude*, and in 1 and 2 *Peter*.

There are various presentations of the Christian application, notably those of Paul, and of the author of the *Epistle to the Hebrews*, who may well have been Apollos of Alexandria (*Acts* xviii.24-26). But we also have certain concepts in *John's Gospel* and the *Revelation*, and of course the Son of Man references in the Synoptic Gospels. On some of these we have touched already, and here we shall mainly be concerned with the Pauline letters and *Hebrews*.

Paul, whose ideas we shall first consider, was quite evidently a master of Jewish mystical teaching, instructed in the *Lore of Creation*. And we may infer both from his language and thought that he had become familiar with certain Essene doctrines while he sojourned in the region of Damascus. It was his great sorrow that the converts he was to make in going to the Gentiles were so physically minded that it was impossible to instruct them in many of the spiritual profundities (*I.Cor*.ii.6-iii.8).

In two passages Paul refers to the Four Matters mentioned in the *Mishnah*,[1] in *Rom*.viii.38-39, and in *Eph*.iii.16-19. We quote the first, where he says: "I am convinced that neither death nor life, neither angels nor ruling spirits, neither Present nor Future, neither Powers Above nor Powers Below, nor anything else which is created, will be able to sever us from the love of God which is in Messiah Jesus our lord."

We have seen that the basics of the Jewish mystical teaching were that the visible universe conforms to a pattern or design, which represents the image of the Invisible God. Man, the crown of creation, being made in the image of God, answers therefore to the original design conceived as a manlike figure, the *Adam Kadmon* or Archetypal Man. We may think of the relationship of the Archetype to God as resembling the relationship between the ideas of an author and himself, and of the human being to the Archetype as the committing of those ideas to writing.

This gives to the creation of man a profound and far-reaching significance in the universal scheme, a significance represented by the Messianic Plan. It was to be deduced, as Paul apprehended, that the Archetypal Man answered to the Messiah Above. In an old Jewish *midrash* we find a like idea. "Thou hast formed me behind and before (*Ps*.cxxxix.5) is to be explained as 'before the first and after the last day of Creation.' For it is said, And the Spirit of the Lord shall rest upon him."[2]

In Paul's words the Messiah (Christ) as Archetypal Man is "the image of the Unseen God, the Firstborn of Creation, that everything in heaven and earth might be founded on him, seen and unseen alike, whether angelic Thrones or Lordships or Rulers or Authorities. Everything was created through him and for him. He is the antecedent of everything, and on him (i.e. as the Archetype) everything was framed. So also is he the Head of the Body, the Community (Church), that is to say, the fount and origin of it, the firstborn from the dead, that in every connection he might take precedence. For it pleased God that by him the whole (i.e. of Creation) should be governed."[3]

Paul's Christ is not God, he is God's first creation, and there is no room for the trinitarian formula of the Athanasian Creed, nor for the doctrine that the Son was "not made, nor created, but begotten." But inasmuch as the visible universe is the self-expression of the Invisible God, so the Messiah, as first-product, is the likeness of that self-expression as *Adam Kadmon*. We can thus appreciate why in *Luke's* Gospel (iii.38) the genealogy is traced back to Adam "who was the son of God."

So Paul writes: "Let your disposition be that of Messiah Jesus, who though he had godlike form (i.e. as Archetypal Man) did not (like the earthly Adam) regard it as a prize to be equal to God (*Gen*.iii.5-6), but divested himself (i.e. put off the garment of light) taking the form of a servant. Appearing in human likeness, and disclosed in physical appearance as a man, he abased himself, and became subject to death, death by the cross. That is why God has so exalted him, that at the name of Jesus every knee, heavenly, earthly and infernal, should bend, and every tongue acclaim Messiah Jesus as lord, to the glory of God the Father."[4]

Here again it is evident that Paul did not think of the Christ Above as God, only as the Archetypal Man, and therefore having a godlike form. Otherwise to be equal with God would have been nothing to grasp at or aspire to. Rather had the Messiah Above while incarnate in Jesus surrendered every attribute of his high estate and become wholly human and devoid of superhumanity. His only special endowment as Jesus was – at his baptism – to receive the gifts of the Spirit (*Isa*.xi.2-3) promised to the Messiah Below.

While on earth Jesus had manifested himself as the True Teacher of the last Times (the Son of Man designate), as according to the Essenes had initially been the case with Enoch. In Jesus the Heavenly Messiah only took over when Jesus was raised from the dead and had ascended to heaven like Enoch (*Rom*.i.4). The heavenly and earthly then became united as the lord Jesus Christ.

Where Paul differed from the Judaeo-Christians and Essenes was in rejecting that the ultimate purpose of God for mankind was the restoration of the Earthly Paradise. He expected the Second Advent to be the means of delivering the saints from the bondage of flesh, and winding up world history. Jesus would return to earth with the angels, but only temporarily, to complete the Messianic purpose. Thereafter God would be all in all (*I.Cor*.xv, *Rom*.viii).

The view of Jesus himself, however, was not like this, but more in accordance with the *Similitudes of Enoch*, where it is said:

And the Lord of Spirits (i.e. God) will abide with them (the Elect), and with that Son of Man will they eat and lie down and rise up for ever and ever. And the righteous and elect will have risen from the earth (by resurrection), and have ceased to be of downcast countenance, and will have been clothed with robes of glory. And these shall be your garments, garments of life before the Lord of Spirits; and your garment shall not grow old and your glory shall not pass away before the Lord of Spirits.[5]

Here the Saints, while redeemed and made immortal, remain distinct from the Heavenly Man, while for Paul they, like Jesus, are amalgamated with him. In the idea of Head and Body this mystery is set out. By a spiritual process completed by their own resurrection the Elect are to grow up until the Body, which is the Community of the Elect, effects a junction with the Head. Jesus and the Elect thereafter will personify the eternal Christ. The spiritual gifts bestowed by the ascension of Jesus were for "the development of the Messianic Body (Body of Christ), until we all reach unity of faith and knowledge of the Son of God, the *perfect Man*, the *measure of the stature of the full-grown Christ*."[6]

The unification of things in heaven and on earth is attained through the Messianic Head which comes down and the Messianic Body which rises up. As it is expressed in the Essenite *Odes of Solomon* (xxiii.14), "the Head went down to the Feet." In the *Odes* (ii.9) the Saint becomes wholly identified with the Heavenly Messiah. Paul expresses this through the husband–wife relationship:

Christ is the head of the Church; and he is the saviour of the body . . . He that loveth his wife loveth himself. For no man ever yet hated his own flesh; but nourisheth and cherisheth it, even as the Lord the Church. For we are members of his body, of his flesh, and of his bones. For this cause shall a man leave his father and mother, and shall be joined unto his wife, and they two shall be one flesh (*Gen*.ii.24). This is a great mystery; but I speak concerning Christ and the Church" (*Eph*.v.22-32).

When the last enemy, Death, has been destroyed there will be no more need for distinctions, since all things Above and Below will have been brought into harmony with God and everything alien or hostile eradicated. At that time the Messianic purpose will be finished, the Grand Design, for which Creation in the Universe was initiated will be complete. There will not be required any longer that there should be the Archetypal Man in a functional capacity, since then "God will be all in all" (*I.Cor*.xv.19-28).

Paul's concept of the Grand Design has not been sufficiently apprehended because those who seek to interpret him have not for the most part been intimate with Jewish esotericism as he was (*Gal*.i.14). Neither has it been recognised, as it should have been, that there are diverse presentations of Christology in the New Testament. The Essene element which appealed to Paul was the age old war, of Zoroastrian origin, of the Messiah with Belial (*II Cor*.vi.15), the war of the Children of Light with the Children of Darkness.[7]

In the *Epistle to the Hebrews* we meet with a still more allegorical presentation, depending partly on the writings of the nearly contemporary Jewish philosopher Philo. The author agrees with Paul that Jesus as a man was totally without divinity.

Since the children have human nature, so did he share it *equally* with them; so that by death he might put out of commission him who wields the power of death, namely the Devil, and release all those inhibited throughout their lives by fear of death. For where was the point of lending a helping hand to angels? It was the offspring of Abraham that needed a helping hand. Consequently it was essential for him to become *in every respect* like his brothers, that he might be a compassionate and trustworthy High Priest in matters relating to God, to propitiate for the people's sins; for having experienced temptation himself he is able to aid those who are tempted.[8]

But we are not concerned here to pursue the developments of Christian doctrine. What we seek to illustrate is the influence of Essene concepts. *Hebrews* is notable in this respect. A legacy from the True Teacher had been the expectation of a Priestly Messiah as well as the Davidic Messiah. Since Christians could only acknowledge one Messiah, the Davidic one, from Judah, it was essential – especially as followers of John the Baptist claimed him as the Priestly Messiah – to establish that Jesus fulfilled the requirements of prophecy in both respects.

The author of *Hebrews* bases his exegesis in Essene fashion on *Psalm* cx: "The Lord said unto my lord (i.e. the king), Sit thou at My right hand, until I make thine enemies thy footstool ... The Lord hath sworn and will not repent, Thou art a priest for ever after the order of Melchizedek."

Jesus, obviously, could not be a priest by descent since he was of the tribe of Judah, not Levi. But he could be the expression of a type of priesthood exercised in Abraham's time by Melchizedek, who was both King of Salem and Priest of the Most High God. What was more, as a type of the Messiah Melchizedek had immortality, "without father, without mother, without ancestry, having neither beginning of days nor end of life" (*Heb.*vii.3).

"Observe, then," our author continues, "what an important person he was to whom Abraham – the Patriarch – gave a tenth of the spoils (*Gen.*xiv.18-20). Those truly of the sons of Levi who possess the priesthood are entitled in accordance with the Law to tithe the people, namely their brothers, although sprung from the loins of Abraham. But this man, not descended from them, has tithed Abraham and blessed the holder of the promises. And beyond all argument it is the inferior who is blessed by the superior. Again, in the one instance it is men subject to death who receive tithes, while in the other (that of Melchizedek) it is on record that he still lives on. As one might put it, through Abraham even Levi, who received tithes, has been tithed, for he was still in his father's loins (of Abraham's grandson Jacob) when Melchizedek met Abraham."[9]

Like the Essenes, the author of *Hebrews* (ch.viii) also sees need in clinching his argument to bring in the promise of a New Covenant. But unlike them, and the Judaeo-Christians, he plays down the idea of the redeemed Earth as the home of the redeemed Elect. "They desire a better country, a heavenly one" (*Heb*.xi.16). He does not see the Messiah reigning in a New Jerusalem, which has come down from heaven, with "the nations of them that are saved walking in the light of it, and the kings of the earth bringing their glory and honour into it" (*Rev*.xxi.24).

# Chapter Twelve

# From Mitra to Maitreya

When we delve into the origins of the Sky Man concept we particularly encounter the figure of the Iranian deity Mitra or Mithra. This is not surprising when we consider that, from the time of Cyrus until Alexander the Great, the Jews had been under Persian rule. Mitra is associated with God, who is Ahura-Mazda, as a projection of Him. He is, as it were, the divine made visible in light, and could thus be symbolised by the sun. In that capacity he was a mediator, a saviour and preserver of mankind, possessed of eternal youth. In the representations of his later cult he is depicted as the slayer of the bull. This has been interpreted as a zodiacal figure, "the sun's entering into the sign of the Bull (Taurus) at the vernal equinox." But also there would seem to have been an age-old reference to the sun as the giver of life, which life is symbolized by blood (*Lev*.xvii.11, etc.). Blood-fertilization of the earth is extremely antique magic. In the Mithra cult the bathing in blood had a redemptive effect.

In the procedure of the Taurobolia and Criobolia, which grew very popular in the Roman world, we have the literal and the original meaning of the phrase 'washed in the blood of the lamb'; the doctrine being that resurrection and eternal life were secured by drenching or sprinkling with the actual blood of a sacrificial bull or ram . . . Thus we have such mortuary inscriptions as *Taurobolio criobolique in aeternum renatus*, 'By the bull-sacrifice and the ram-sacrifice born again for eternity.'[1]

In his solar representation Mithra had the festival of his birthday on December 25th, "the birthday of the invincible sun," which the Church found appropriate to take over as the birthday of Jesus i.e. Christmas. At the vernal equinox there was also a confusion between the death and resurrection of Jesus and Mithraic ritual tribute to the revival of nature in the springtime. The likenesses to Christian doctrine were so obvious and awkward that they were held by the Church Fathers to have been the work of the Devil. Thus, with reference to the Last Supper, we find that Justin Martyr in the second century A.D. accuses the demon of having wilfully imitated the Christian rites in the mysteries of Mithra, "commanding the same things to be done. For, that bread and a cup of water are placed with certain incantations in the mystic rites of one who is being initiated, you can either known or can learn."[2]

The Church Father Tertullian, a little later, had an even more detailed knowledge of Mithraism, and no less believed that "the Devil, by the mysteries of his idols, imitates even the main part of the divine mysteries . . . There Mithra sets his mark on the foreheads of his soldiers; he celebrates the oblation of bread: he offers an image of the resurrection, and presents at once the crown and the sword; he limits his chief priests to a single marriage: he even has his virgins and his ascetics (continentes)."[3]

But it was chiefly in his solar aspect that Mithra made his appeal to the Essenes and other Jewish mystics. Before there was light there could be no creation, since without it the visible could not proceed from the invisible. As the great luminary, the sun, therefore, was a reflection of the glory of God and of His life-giving power, and also of the force of Good over against darkness as the force of Evil. It is easy to see what an impression Iranian dualistic faith made on Jewish thinkers from the sixth to the fourth century B.C.

Josephus refers to the solar symbolism of the Essenes. "Before the sun is up they utter no word of mundane matters, but offer to him certain prayers, which have been handed down from their fore-fathers, as though entreating him to rise."[4] From the Essenes the early Christians identified Jesus as the incarnation of the Messiah Above who was a Being of Light, the "king from the sun" who would deliver the world from evil.

Pliny the Younger wrote to the Emperor Trajan about the Christians (c. 112 A.D.) that "they met on a certain day before it was light and sang an antiphonal chant to Christ as to a god."[5] Very probably this was the antiphonal hymn with which the Gospel of John opens, where the Logos is hailed as the True Light, which illumines all who enter the world. Thus, like Solomon son of David, described as son of God, the Messianic son of David could be hailed as the Sun-King.[6]

Here we are back in the realm of Sky Man, the Light-Adam of the Mandaeans and the Jewish mystics, the Son of Man represented by the antediluvian Enoch after his translation to heaven, "whose flesh was turned to flame, his veins to fire, his eye-lashes to flashes of lightning, his eye-balls to flaming torches, and whom God placed on a throne next to the throne of glory."[7] We are not surprised, therefore, to find Enoch in his heavenly significance accorded certain aspects and functions of Mithra (Mitra), and accordingly by the Jewish mystics being called Metatron (Meetatron).[8]

Delving into Rabbinical teaching the figure of the heavenly being Metatron, the Prince of the Presence, bears much the same relationship to God as Mithra does to Ahura-Mazda in the Iranian teaching. Mithra was God in self-expression, preserver of mankind from the Evil One, mediator between God and Man.

Of Metatron we learn: "His office of Advocate of Israel (i.e. with God) is clearly brought out in (the Talmud) *Chagigah* 15a, where he is represented as writing down, in the presence of God, the merits of the Children of Israel; he is thus spoken of as the 'Great Scribe', the advocate who pleads on behalf of his clients before the Judge. In (the Midrash) *Bemidbar Rabbah*, c.12, the term 'Mediator' is directly applied to Metatron, and, what is still more significant, he is represented as the reconciler between God and the Chosen People."[9]

There is a noted passage in the Babylonian Talmud[10] where a Rabbi is rebutting the contention of a Min (heretic) that there are two Powers in heaven, God and His likeness.

R.Nachman said, 'He who knows how to answer the Minim like R.Idi, let him answer; if not, let him not answer.' A certain Min said to R.Idi, 'It is written (*Exod.* xxiv. 1), *And He said unto Moses, Come up unto the Lord*. He ought to have said, *Come up unto Me*.' He (i.e. R.Idi) said, 'This is Metatron, whose name is as the name of his Master. For it is written (*Exod.* xxiii. 21), *For My name is in him*.' 'If so, worship him' (urged the Min). 'But it is also written (the Rabbi responded), *Provoke him not* i.e. Do not mistake him for Me)'.

With such mystical notions of God in *Being*, and God in *Expression*, there was a very grave risk of compromising the Unity of God. There was the same problem with the concept of the relationship between God and His Word (*Memra*). Christianity in its development opted for a doctrine of the deity of Christ, as did certain Gnostics. Some Jewish esotericists were sorely tempted to compromise the Divine Unity, and often strayed very close to the border line. A few succumbed.

One of the victims was the famous Rabbi Elisha ben Abuyah, one of the four Jewish sages of the second century A.D. who are said to have entered Paradise, that is, in their case, to have reached a high stage of initiation into the heavenly mysteries. There Elisha saw Metatron "to whom is given the permission to *sit* in order to record the merits of Israel." But surely no one could be seated in heaven, not even the angels, only God himself! Were there, then, Elisha considered, Two Powers in heaven? To contradict such an impious infe.'ence, the angels brought out Metatron and gave him sixty strokes with a lash of fire. [11]

It is fascinating to delve into these matters, but we must not stray too far from our theme in its essential elements. Behind all these concepts is a human faith that man is not the product of chance. He has a purpose and a destiny, of which he has been made partially aware. Like all great enterprises of a radical nature his is attended by grave risks. Man must even be tempted to fail, and urged to give up the struggle, so that his task is all the harder and he is brought close to despair.

But still man can be conscious that he is intended to succeed, and has not been left to rely solely on his very limited resources. Not only can he receive inspiration; he can be encouraged by the power of an outstanding example and the presence of an exalted helping hand related to his own nature. "A second Adam to the fight, and to the rescue came." Man can know that at the core he is of the stuff that brought the universe into being. He is the microcosm of which Sky Man is the macrocosm. In the time of man's greatest need and peril, when he is on the brink of disaster, Sky Man will be there.

Yes, but there is also a sense in which he is always among us unrecognised, sharing our trials, setting us an example, lending us a helping hand, enduring the worst that can befall us. He can turn up anywhere, in the guise of a beggar or tramp, as a travelling sage or pilgrim, as the True Teacher, as the Wandering Jew. We have built our legends on this deep-seated theme from far back in the human story, and continue to do so in this technological age in our film creations whose mechanics give a startling verisimilitude to the bogus miraculous. We continue to recognise, as Abraham did, that we should be kind to the stranger, for we may be entertaining an angel unaware.

And always there is the stimulus of looking forward to a goal, the climax, the triumph, the victory of life over death, the justification on the testing-ground of our planet of all the suffering and the agony. No wonder the doctrine of Reincarnation was conceived in the harsh and crushing East. From Mitra and Metatron to Messiah and Maitreya the Hope is passed on.

It is in Buddhism that we find an expectation comparable to Jewish

Messianism, and partly derived from it. This is why it has been so easy to effect interchange between traditions of the Buddha and of Jesus, and through a Joasaph to discover links with the Essenes and their True Teacher.

The Lord Maitreya (i.e. Mitra-Metatron) is to be the last incarnation of the Buddha, awaited especially by many monks in Tibet and Mongolia. It is said that on the rocks of many mountains is inscribed, "Come, Maitreya, come!"[12]

The Buddha foretold the Golden Age of the world, when as predicted,

The inhabitants will commit no crime or evil deeds, but will take pleasure in doing good. The soil will then be free from thorns, even, and covered with a fresh green growth of grass ... Rich silken, and other fabrics of various colours shoot forth from the trees. The trees will bear leaves, flowers, and fruits simultaneously ... Human beings are then without blemish, moral offences are unknown among them, and they are full of zest and joy ...

After this:

Maitreya, the best of men, will then leave the Tushita heavens, and go for his last rebirth into the womb of the woman [Brahmavati, wife of the Brahmin Subrahmana]. For ten whole months she will carry about his radiant body. Then she will go to a grove full of beautiful flowers and there, neither seated nor lying down, but standing up, holding on to the branch of a tree, she will give birth to Maitreya. He, supreme among men, will emerge from her right side, as the sun shines forth when it has prevailed over a bank of clouds ... He will fill this entire Triple world with his splendour ... He will raise his voice to the ten directions,[13] and will speak these words: 'This is my last birth. There will be no rebirth after this one. Never will I come back here, but, all pure, I shall win Nirvana!'

And when his father sees that his son has the Thirty-two Marks of a superman ... he will be filled with joy ... Maitreya will have a heavenly voice which reaches far; his skin will have a golden hue, a great splendour will radiate from his body, his chest will be broad, his limbs well developed, and his eyes will be like lotus petals. His body is eighty cubits high, and twenty cubits broad ... And then, a supreme sage, he will with a perfect voice preach the true dharma, which is auspicious and removes all ill ...[14]

This conception, as we can see, has points of contact with the Messianic mysticism of Essenes, Jews and Christians. We note especially the height of Maitreya, as of Adam before he sinned, when he was a being of light. He bears the 32 marks of superhumanity, answering to the 10 *Sejiroth* plus the 22 letters of the Hebrew alphabet of the Jewish mystics, the "thirty-two secret paths of wisdom" through which God has created all that exists.[15]

### Chapter Thirteen

# More Things in Heaven and Earth

We have travelled far afield in following ancient ideas which the Essenes made their own, and wove into the rich fabric of the Messianic. What they created was to be an inspiration to millions in many lands, in many centuries, under the auspices of different faiths.

I cannot know what you, the reader, have gained from this exploration. But I hope you have felt something of the impact of the infinite on the finite, of that which has inspired us earthlings to reach for the stars and beyond, against all odds and despite all obstacles. I trust that you now have a better understanding of the real nature of the Messianic, which I may broadly define as the philosophy of the Eternal Incentive. It has its emblem in the Jewish symbol, the so-called Shield of David, with its interlocking triangles, the one aimed downward from above and the other aimed upward from below.

The Messianic, as the sages of old saw it, was already present when our world came into being. I give here my own rendering of the opening verses of *Genesis* in the Bible in the root significance of the Hebrew text.

> First of all God created heaven and earth.
> But earth was featureless and creatureless,
> And a stillness lay upon the surface of the deep.
> Only the Wind of God ruffled the surface of the waters.
> Then God said, 'Let there be a stirring!'
> And a stirring took place.
> And God contemplated the stirring and found it good.
> So God distinguished stirring-time from still-time.
> Stirring-time He called Day, and still-time Night.
> Thus passive and active was One Day.

The Wind, or Spirit, of God, declared the Rabbis, is the Spirit of the Messiah. It is a very simple and engaging imagery; but it brings out the idea that the impetus to activity was there from the beginning, and no one can say when the drum beats of pulsating being first began to sound. The Messianic marks the intrusion of gusts of the fresh, the clean and the pure, dispersing the miasma of the stagnant and foul, overcoming death by the perpetual reassertion of life.

The legacy of the True Teacher has also provided us with another aspect of the Messianic as apprehended by the Essenes, the aspect which carried through the ages the struggle between the forces of Good and Evil. This had largely been taken over from Iranian and even older speculations.

We still preserve reflections of this conflict in the world of fairy-tale, where the good fairy counters the schemes of the evil magician or wicked witch. It is always the goodies versus the baddies. And elements in the struggle are the peril and suffering of the humans involved. There is the aim of 'evil' to prevent the 'poor mortals' accomplishing their task, and the aim of 'good' which is to enable them to press on to ultimate victory. At the end is the Golden Age, when they live happily ever after.

And there is often another element in the story, an element with which we have been engaged in this volume, which is the testing of the humans through their feeling of kindness and compassion. The 'good' manifests itself in legend in the guise of an ugly old crone or a blind beggar. Will the mortals prove deserving of redemption? Only when they have exhibited their compassion and concern is it revealed who the unprepossessing visitor really is. Sometimes we have a human – a prince – who abandons the pleasure and luxury of his father's palace to make a home with the downtrodden and the destitute. At other times, in an area of conflict and grave perils, of anger and strife, a mysterious and nameless stranger appears to put things right. When all is resolved and the stranger is to be warmly thanked it is found that he has disappeared as unnoticed as when he came. Our modern world has created its own fantasy of figures of Good and Evil to serve the same purposes, and does so all the more whenever the struggle appears to be intensifying.

In the most outstanding of the previous 'Last Times' periods Messianic faith made the impact which has been with us – though largely misunderstood – for the past two thousand years. What impact will it make on what promises to be the 'Last Times' period which has now begun?

In all such ways as we have mentioned, and there are others, something in us is seeking to take hold of and express our confidence that it is not by chance that we are in this world, that through our being here we are making a contribution – however humble – to the fulfilment of some tremendous and unimaginable destiny, and that our participation is an essential part of that destiny.

Deep down, something in us seems to be striving to make the bold and the seemingly presumptuous assertion that we are identified with Sky Man, that we bear his likeness, and that accordingly our function is Cosmic. And who is to say we are wrong? Perhaps all the galaxies are but organisms in the body of the universe, which we are observing only from the inside.

In this context we have thought, perhaps mistakenly, of Sky Man having reduced himself to our dimensions to bring us inspiration and relief. Instead, we should have been making the tremendous affirmation that we were an infinitesimal and yet integral part of him, and thus able to draw upon him in time of need in order to fulfil our function. Close to this has been the idea of the Elect as Son of Man, as the proof of his Messianic presence, and attuned to the fulfilment of his function to save Society. In this respect the Chosen People were to be the living evidence of his presence, and the means of mankind's salvation.

Jesus, as a Jew oriented to the Messianic, put this very well on one occasion, when he was asked to state when the Kingdom of God would appear. He replied, "The Kingdom of God will not come by keeping a sharp look-out for it. Nor is it going to be said, 'Here it is!' or 'There it is!' – for the Kingdom of God is right beside you."[1]

The Essenes could see in their True Teacher, as others have done with other Teachers, a special Sky Man impetus to which we could respond in time of crisis or emergency. In that assurance we are to accept our strivings and vicissitudes as linked with the stars in an unfathomable glorious enterprise. To quote the words of the Teacher:

> Always,
>     at the genesis of every period,
>     and at the beginning of every age,
>     and at the end of every season,
> according to the statute and signs,
>     appointed to every dominion,
>     by the certain law from the mouth of God,
> by the precept which is and which shall be
>     for ever and ever without end.
> Without it nothing is nor shall be,
>     for the God of knowledge establishes it,
>     for there is no other beside Him.[2]

# The Essenes and the Templars

When I had completed the major part of the text of this work some information about the Knights Templar became available. As this was both relevant and of special interest I have thought it well to present it in an Appendix.

The information has been gleaned from a recent book entitled *The Holy Blood and the Holy Grail*, written by Michael Baigent, Richard Leighton and Henry Lincoln, and published in the United Kingdom by Jonathan Cape. The theme of the authors is largely unrelated to my own, and one which I am not able to support. But their researches turned up information which in important aspects comes into conjunction with it. So it is fortunate for me that their volume should have made such a timely appearance.

In the course of their researches the authors had need to investigate and cite ancient sources relating to the Templars, some of which – as I could judge – had positive links with Essenism. Accordingly, I have been very thankful to be given access to this material and to be able to utilise it. Happily, I am in a position to reciprocate with disclosures which have a relevance to these authors' own inquiries. References to their book are cited by the initials *HBHG* with page numbers.

The military Order of the Knights Templar was founded, according to Guillaume de Tyre, in 1118 A.D. by a certain nobleman of Champagne called Hugues de Payen. The full title of the Order was that of the Poor Knights of Christ and the Temple of Solomon, and it originally consisted of nine knights including the founder. The second half of the title derived from the circumstance that initially the building the Templars occupied formed part of the ancient Jewish Temple at Jerusalem.

The declared purpose of the Order, as stated by Guillaume de Tyre, was, "as far as their strength permitted, they should keep the roads and highways (i.e. of the Holy Land) safe ... with especial regard for the protection of pilgrims."[1]

The Templars, however, were to become noted in other ways, as

repositories of unorthodox and esoteric teachings. The authors of
*HBHG* state that they had a "sustained and sympathetic contact with
Islamic and Jewish culture."[2] This is very important, as it enabled
them to gain access to some of the methods and mysteries of Eastern
occultism.

Moreover the Templars had an increasingly intimate relationship
with the Cathars, especially in south-western Europe in the
Languedoc, and many Cathar nobles enrolled in the Order. We are
informed that:

By virtue of their contact with Islamic and Jewish cultures, the Templars had
already absorbed a great many ideas alien to orthodox Roman Christianity.
Templar Masters, for example, often employed Arab secretaries, and many
Templars, having learnt Arabic in captivity, were fluent in the language. A
close rapport was also maintained with Jewish communities, financial
interests and scholarship. The Templars had thus been exposed to many
things Rome would not ordinarily countenance. Through the influx of
Cathar recruits, they were now exposed to Gnostic dualism as well – if,
indeed, they had ever really been strangers to it.

Through these associations the Templars would have been able to
gain access to much Essene teaching, as latterly channelled through
Gnostic and Kabbalistic concepts. These esoteric matters could only
be pursued by the Templars in secret and under strict pledges of
silence. But they changed the whole character of the Order; and it
could not fail to get around through leaks and rumours that the
power of the Templars had come to reside in arts and knowledge
reputedly sinister.

The Cathars, as we know, held the book *Barlaam and Joasaph* in
high repute, and some of the Asaph texts had reached the West in the
Middle Ages. As regards Gnostic dualism, which influenced the
Cathars, this had positive Essene antecedents. The *Odes of Solomon*
have been held to have been a product of Valentinian Gnosticism,
and among them we have found a psalm which compares with the
*Thanksgiving Psalms* among the Dead Sea Scrolls, which are considered by some scholars to have been the work of the mysterious
True Teacher.

From the evidences that have survived can we penetrate further
the arcane secrets of the Templars?

At the beginning of the fourteenth century Philippe IV of France
in his own interests proceeded against the Templars, having enlisted
the co-operation of the Pope, Clement V.

"In France the arrested Templars were tried and many subjected to torture. Strange confessions were extracted and even stranger accusations made. Grim rumours began to circulate about the country. The Templars supposedly worshipped a devil called Baphomet. At their secret ceremonies they supposedly prostrated themselves before a bearded male head, which spoke to them and invested them with occult powers. Unauthorised witnesses of these ceremonies were never seen again."[4]

The mysteries here referred to have never been explained. But the evidences of links with Essene lore suggested to me that these reports might have a foundation in fact. I decided to treat the obviously artificial name Baphomet as another case of the use of the Hebrew Atbash cipher for purposes of concealment. Setting down Baphomet in Hebrew characters produced בפומת|, which by Atbash converted immediately into שופיא| (Sophia), the Greek word for Wisdom (|Σοφία). So this centuries old secret was for the first time revealed!

But what about the bearded male head? In the cosmic figure of the Adam Kadmon (Sky Man) the bearded male head is denominated in Hebrew as חכמה| (Chokmah), i.e. Wisdom.[5] The Greek Sophia represents a female rather than a male, and we are not surprised to find in Templar hands, according to Inquisition records, a casket surmounted by "a great head of gilded silver, most beautiful, and constituting the image of a woman."[6]

It would seem that the Templars, whether through the Cathars or independently, had access to Gnostic mythology which in turn had derived from extremely ancient cosmological interpretations. In the Bible there is an echo in *Proverbs* viii, where Wisdom (feminine), like the masculine Logos (Word) of *John's Gospel*, was in the Beginning with God, and beside Him when He created the Earth. But in *Proverbs* Wisdom is contrasted with Folly, represented in the previous chapter by a harlot. Whereas in the Gnostic systems Wisdom was captured by the Powers of the material world and forced to prostitute herself. It was to redeem her, and thus "restore all things", that the Archetypal Man appeared on Earth.[7]

The Simonian (Simon Magus) doctrine equated Sophia with Ennoia (the First Thought) of God. According to a Gnostic hymn:

> She passed from body to body,
> Always suffering disgrace from it;
> Last of all
> She was manifest in a prostitute;
> This is the lost sheep.
> For her sake He came,

To free her from her bonds,
And to offer men salvation
Through their recognition of him.[8]

Simon Magus claimed to have discovered this 'lost sheep' in a prostitute in Tyre called Helen, and went about with her, he as the Sun and she as the Moon (Selene = Luna). There is much we could go into here, but it would take us too much off course. We may note, however, that the pagan side of the Gnostic myth is that the Simonians worshipped Helen as Athena (Goddess of Wisdom), who in turn was identified in Egypt with Isis. Plutarch states that Isis was sometimes called Sophia,[9] and in a papyrus from Oxyrhynchus Isis is identified with Syrian Astarte. We can, indeed, go much further back to "the old Babylonian goddess Inanna, the one who descended to the lower world and was mistreated at its seven gates."[10]

There would seem to be little doubt that the beautiful woman's head of the Templars represents Sophia in her female and Isis aspect, and she was linked with Mary Magdalene in the Christian interpretation. The mythological and cosmic origins would seem to have been known to an appreciable extent by the Templars. *HBHG*, among its illustrations, depicts the seal of the British branch of the Order in 1303 A.D.[11] The symbolism is disguised cosmic and inter-faith. At the top the star and crescent of Islam has been adapted by depicting the crescent moon of the Mother Goddess as a boat with the cross pattée on a pole serving as the mast. Underneath is a lion, ostensibly of England, but actually the Lion of the Sun and of Judah (the king from the sun). On either side are single five-pointed stars, conceivably representing the twin Messianic functions, Priestly and Regal, like the two olive trees of *Zech*.iv.11-14. The symbolism is very close to the Messianic Mystery as conceived by the Essenes.

## Appendix B

# Out of Egypt

Ancient Egypt was a land which lent itself physically and spiritually to a variety of religious experiences and disciplines. Its heart-beat of the rise and fall of the Nile gave life to its cities, to be built of its resources of stone, while its fringe of deserts under its star-lit skies lent themselves to meditation and the contemplation of eternity. The mingling of peoples and cultures increased here from period to period, shaping relationships and new philosophies. Above all, Egypt was the natural home of mysteries and mysticism.

Particularly within the period from 400 B.C. to 200 A.D. Egypt had become the melting pot of the ancient world. On the foundations of its ancient faith had been imposed superstructures introduced by alien rulers, Medo-Persian, Greek and Roman, while there had been an increasingly strong Jewish influence. As a consequence there were religious fusions and amalgamations, and the emergence of spiritual hybrids. Isis and Athena joined forces. Osiris and Apis blended into Serapis. Zoroastrianism and Mithraism lent their characteristics to Jewish Essenic teaching, and found a Greek expression in the Hermetic and Christian Gnostic. The coverage of the Roman Empire right round the Mediterranean carried the cults with it, and opened the way for new blendings. Another wave would sweep across with the later advances of militant Islam. Thus the mystical secret societies of Europe could and did look back to Egypt, and especially to Alexandria, as their ancestral home.

The influence of the Essenes of Egypt, known in the first century A.D. as Therapeuts, was particularly strong. Philo of Alexandria learned much from them. The Rosicrucians could look back to an Essene impetus from Egypt relating to arcane matters associated with the Sun-King and Master of Wisdom King Solomon, who had created the Temple in conjunction with the Master Asaph ben Berechiah. And these things were the foundations of Freemasonry.

For information on these aspects I am most grateful to an American friend Mr Livingston Dodson, who has drawn my attention to the material contained in a work published in Paris in 1815 entitled *Acta Latomorum, ou Chronologie de L'Histoire de La Franche-Maçonnerie Française et Étrangère*. Speaking of the Alexandrian developments the author tells us, and I translate, "Around the same time, the Essenes and other Jews founded a School of Solomonic Wisdom, which reunited with Ormus. The Society later divided into a variety of Orders known under the term Conservers of the Mosaic Secrets, the Hermetic Secrets, etc." (pp.336–337).

Speaking of another order of Freemasonry, the same author tells us that "the sectaries pretend that the Grand Master is in Spain, where he is designated by the name *Tajo*" (p.294). What he did not realise, but we now can in the light of the Atbash cipher, is that the Spanish *Tajo*, pronounced TACHO, converts by Atbash into ASAPH. TACHO is from the Greek TAXO of the book *Assumption of Moses*, which marked the beginning of our quest.

# Notes and References

INTRODUCTION

1. J.M. Allegro, *The Dead Sea Scrolls*, Pelican Books (1956), p.47.
2. By Michael Baigent, Richard Leigh and Henry Lincoln (*Jonathan Cape*), 1982. And see below, Appendix A.


PART ONE
CHAPTER ONE

1. Josephus, *Jewish War*, II.145.
2. *Testaments of the XII Patriarchs*, Levi XVI.1-5.
3. John Hyrcanus, the most prominent of the Priestly Hasmonean rulers, was hailed as heir to the triple attributes, and assumed the title given to the Biblical Melchizedek (*Gen.xiv.*18) Priest of the Most High God. Accordingly, though Jesus was of the tribe of Judah the endeavour was made to present him in the *Epistle to the Hebrews* as Priest of the Order of Melchizedek.


CHAPTER TWO

1. Or True Teacher.
2. *Hosea* iv.16.
3. The curses are those of *Deut.*xxviii.15-26.
4. *Fragments of a Zadokite Work*, [8].15-17 (Tr. from the Hebrew by R.H. Charles.) The original MSS are at Cambridge University.
5. *I.Macc.* 1.10-15, 62-64, and cp. *Dan.*1.8.
6. The first visitation brought about the Babylonian Exile in the 6th century B.C.
7. *Assumption of Moses* (Tr. R.H. Charles). The first paragraph quoted is from the close of ch.viii, due to a transposition of part of the text made deliberately by a Christian scribe. Originally ch.viii directly followed ch.v. In the quotations I have abridged part of the text. The omissions are represented by ...
8. Cp. *II.Cor.*vi.14-15, *Lk.*xvi.8, *I.Thess.*v.5, *Rev.*xii.7.
9. For references to the Poor see *Lk.*vi.20, *Rom.*xv.26, *Gal.*ii.10, and *Jas.*ii.5. The first Christian Community began with the members giving away all their possessions, *Acts* ii.44-45, v.1-4. This followed the Essene practice.


CHAPTER THREE

1. *II Macc.*IV.12-15.
2. For more on Alcimus see the next chapter.
3. *II.Macc.*XIV.6-10.
4. On the significance of this quotation see below Part One Ch vii.
5. An alternative version of the death of Alcimus is given in the next chapter.

## CHAPTER FOUR

1. The first visitation was that of the Babylonian Exile in the time of Nebuchadnezzar. See above p.20.
2. *Assumption of Moses*, IX (Tr. R.H. Charles).
3. See above p.9, and also below p.45.
4. See above p.21.
5. Above p.21 and Part One, chapter 5.
6. *Mishnah, Chag.*ii.7.
8. *Genesis Rabba*, XV.22.

## CHAPTER FIVE

1. See below Pt.1, ch.x. The theme of the New Covenant is applied to Jesus in *Hebrews* viii.
2. See below pp.72-73.
3. See *Jewish Encyclopaedia* (Funk & Wagnalls), article JOSEPH.
4. Above p.33.
5. Above p.18.
6. Cp. the saying attributed to Jesus on the cross (*Lk.*xxiii.34), "Father forgive them; for they know not what they do."
7. *Test.Benj.*iii.1-8.
8. *Ascension of Isaiah*, edited and translated by R.H. Charles, p.39.
9. *Test. Simeon*, viii.1-2.

## CHAPTER SIX

1. *Bab.Mets.*114b.Ritual defilement would be incurred for a priest.
2. *Midr.Tehill.*xliii.1.
3. *Ecclus.*xlviii.10.
4. On *Num.*xxv.12.
5. *Pirke de R. Eliezer*,xxix, xlvii; *Biblical Antiquities of Philo*, xlviii.
6. Dupont-Sommer, *The Jewish Sect of Qumran and the Essenes*, p.76.
7. See below Part 2, ch.ix
8. See Part 1, ch.x.
9. Epiphanius, *Haeres.*lxxviii. James the brother of Jesus was greatly exalted by the Judaeo-Christians. But Epiphanius was citing legends built up from the information that he regularly visited the Temple to pray for the people.
10. Josephus, *Antiq.* Bk.xx.200.
11. *Sidra d'Yahya*, sect.18.
12. Ephraim, *Gospel Commentaries*. A reading to the same effect is found in the Gospel MS. Codex Algerinae Peckover. See also Hippolytus of Rome, *Comm. on the Blessings of Isaac, Jacob and Moses*.
13. See Part 1, ch.viii.
14. Moses Gaster, *Samaritan Eschatology*.
15. *Gen.*xxx.23-24

## CHAPTER SEVEN

1. See Introduction p. 9. The passage relating to Taxo is quoted in full on p.32-33 above.
2. Rappoport, *Myth and Legend of Ancient Israel*, Vol.III, pp.97, 200, 204.
3. Manetho, quoted by Josephus *Against Apion*.
4. See further below Bk.1, ch.viii.

5. G. Vermes, *The Dead Sea Scrolls in English*, p.149.
6. See J. Teicher, *Journal of Jewish Studies*, Vol.II, No.2, p.89f.


## CHAPTER EIGHT

1. Tr.H.St.J.Thackeray, (*Loeb Classical Library* edition).
2. See *J.E.* article *Asaph ben Berechiah*, Vol.II,p.162, and A.Mingana, *Some Judaeo-Christian Documents in the John Rylands Library*, pp.20–21.
3. A.Mingana, *op.cit.* pp.20–29.
4. See below, Part One, chs.xi and xii.
5. See above p.41.
6. See above p.43.
7. *The Oath of Asaph the Physician and Yochanan ben Zabda*, The Israel Academy of Sciences and Humanities Proceedings, Vol.v, No.9, 1975.
8. Schonfield, *Saints Against Caesar*.
9. *On the Contemplative Life* (Tr.F.H.Colson), Philo, vol.ix (Loeb Classical Library).
10. *Aboda Zara*, 27b.
11. *Shabbath*, 14b.
12. *Sanhedrin*, x.1.
13. *Journal of Biblical Literature*, Vol.xii, pp.122–124.
14. Epiphanius, *Panarion*, xxx.
15. JE. art. *Asaph ben Berechiah*.


## CHAPTER NINE

1. *Matt.*xxiii.34–35. In *Luke* xi.49-50 the name of Zechariah's father is not given, and the saying is treated as a quotation by Jesus from the *Wisdom of God*.
2. *Jewish War*, IV.334-334.
3. *TJ.Taanith*, 69a-b, and *TB.Sanhedrin*, 96b.
4. The Courts referred to formed part of the structure of the Temple at Jerusalem, of which the Court of the Priests was the inner court.
5. Edited and translated from two Syriac MSS by Dr.A.Mingana, *Bulletin of the John Rylands Library*, Manchester, July 1927.
6. The theme of the birth stories relating to John the Baptist, was explored by the present writer as far back as 1929 in his book *The Lost Book of the Nativity of John*, T.& T.Clark, Edinburgh. An English translation of the John passages in the Mandaean texts will be found in *The Gnostic John the Baptizer*, by G.R.S.Mead, published by John M.Watkins, London, 1924.


## CHAPTER TEN

1. See above pp.41.
2. *The Gospel of Thomas*, [II] (82.25-30), (Tr.William R. Schoedel). See *The Secret Sayings of Jesus*, by Grant and Freedman.
3. See Jerone, *Catal.Script.Eccl.* (under *Jacobus*). The appearance of Jesus to Jacob was later according to *I.Cor.*xv.7.
4. Eusebius, *Eccl.Hist.*,Bk.II.iii.
5. Presumably Pharisees, and possibly Essenes also.
6. Josephus, *Antiquities* Bk.xx.200-203.
7. Hegesippus, *Memoirs*, Bk. 5, quoted by Euseb. *Eccl.Hist.*, Bk.II.xxiii.
8. Origin, *Contra Cels.*, Bk.I.xlvii.

### CHAPTER ELEVEN

1. The Christian Scriptures employ this concept of the New Covenant in *Hebrews* viii in association with the attribution to Jesus of high priesthood. And of course New Testament is a version of New Covenant.
2. See the *Damascus Document*, viii.1-10, ix.10-29 (Tr.R.H. Charles, *Fragments of a Zadokite Work*, 1912); and further see below the next chapter.
3. Among the finds at the Essene site at Qumran was the famed copper scroll, which catalogues places of concealment of treasures and various materials which may have come from the Temple at Jerusalem in the first century A.D.
4. See Moses Gaster, *Samaritan Eschatology*, and Josephus, *Antiq*.XVIII.85-86; and above p.42.
6. *Secrets of the Dead Sea Scrolls*, ch.ii, pp.8-9 (first published in 1956 and now out of print).
7. It is to be noted that there is a denunciation of Edom and Babylon in *Ps*.cxxxvii, which psalm in the Greek version is attributed to the Prophet Jeremiah.
8. *Jubilees*,xlv.16.

### CHAPTER TWELVE

1. "From Aaron," that is from the priests and Levites.
2. *Damascus Document*,viii.1-10.
3. Josephus, *Jewish War*,II.145, and see above p.17 and *Jn*.i.21.
4. Cp. the use by Jacob (James) of the same passage of *Amos* in Acts xv.14-17.
5. The Essene expositor interprets the 'coming forth' as a going forth from the Land of Israel.
6. *Damascus Document*, ix.4-9.
7. *Damascus Document*, ix.19-20.
8. *Damascus Document*, ix.46-47.
9. See above Ch.3, pp.28-29.
10. My rendering is taken from J.M. Allegro, 'Further Light on the History of the Qumran Sect' (*Journal of Biblical Literature*). The defects in the manuscript have given rise to alternative dealings with the lacunae by scholars, as for example by G.Vermes, *The Dead Sea Scrolls in English*, p.23 1f and 58f. However, the crucial sentence about Demetrius is not affected. It is only a question of which Demetrius was intended that is a matter of opinion.
11. Josephus, *Antiq*. Bk.xiii.1-5.
12. *Damascus Document*, v.6-vi.3.
13. *Ps.Sol*.xvii.16-19 (Tr.J.Rendel Harris, *The Odes & Psalms of Solomon*).
14. *Damascus Document*,ix.28 (Text B).
15. *Damascus Document*,ix.36-37.

### CHAPTER THIRTEEN

1. Philo, *Contemplative Life* (65), notes the special observation of the Feast of Pentecost by the Therapeuts of Egypt.
2. *Community Rule*, II.
3. *Community Rule*, I-II (Tr.G.Vermes), *The Dead Sea Scrolls in English*, p.44.
4. See *Acts* iv.34-v.II.
5. See above Ch.x.
6. See Schonfield, *The Jew of Tarsus*.

## CHAPTER FOURTEEN

1. *Isa*.xi.31; *Mal*.iii.1.
2. See above p.70-71.
3. The passage follows Bk.II.110 of the *Jewish War*, and is given in full in the Appendix to Thackeray's translation in the Loeb Classical Library edition of Josephus. See also Eisler, *The Messiah Jesus and John the Baptist*.
4. *Acts* xxii. Ananias, like an Essene, speaks obliquely of the Just One, and does not utter his personal name.
5. Josephus, *Jewish War*,I.398.
6. *Antiquities*,XVII¡23-27.
7. Pliny, *Natural History*, v.81.
8. *Jewish War*,III.542.
9. *Tosephta, Shabbath* xiii.5.
10. *B.Shabb.*116. The Talmudic passages quoted, with others which are relevant, may be consulted in R.T. Hertford, *Christianity in Talmud and Midrash* (Williams & Norgate, 1903).
11. *B.Sotah*, 47.
12. See above p.73.
13. Macuch, *Alter und Heimat der Mandäismus nach neuerschlossenen Quellen* (Theologische Literaturzeitung, 82). See also Matthew Black, *The Scrolls and Christian origins*, p.68.
14. E.S.Drower, *Mandaean Polemic*, Bulletin of the School of Oriental and African Studies, Vol.xxv, Part 3, 1962.
15. See above, chapter viii, The Legacy of Shem.

## CHAPTER FIFTEEN

1. See above p.83.
2. Epiphanius, *Panarion* (Against Heresies), Vol.1.xxix. Ed.Francis Oehler.
3. J.Parkes, *The Conflict of the Church and the Synagogue*, p.398.
4. Parkes, *Op.cit.*, p.301.
5. See Schonfield, *According to the Hebrews*.
6. For the information given I am indebted to Shlomo Pines, *The Jewish Christians of the Early Centuries of Christianity according to a New Source* (Proceedings of the Israel Academy of Sciences and Humanities, Vol.II, No.13).
7. The texts used by 'Abd al-Jabbar not only refer several times to Harran, they mention persecutions there instigated by the Emperor Constantine. They even claim that his 'wife' Helena had worked in an inn there.
8. As he appears in the Clementine *Homilies* and *Recognitions*.
9. See above Part One, ch.vii, and on Jeremiah ch.xi.
10. H.Gregoire, *Les Gens de la Caverne, les Qaraites et les Khazars*, i. *Le Flambeau*, Brussels, 1952, has pointed out that the Karaite work known as the *Cambridge Anonymous*, has inserted into the history of the conversion of the Khazars to Judaism a passage referring to the discovery of Hebrew MSS in a cave.
11. S.Schechter, *Documents of Jewish Sectaries*, Vol.1.
12. See above Part One, chs.vii and viii. Naturally we cannot directly relate the one circumstance to the other, but the approximate dates obtainable are very close.

PART TWO

CHAPTER ONE

1. Eisler, *The Messiah Jesus and John the Baptist*, p.157.
2. Eisler, *op.cit.*
3. Eisler, *op.cit.*, p.165.
4. See above, p.51.
5. For the foregoing information I am particularly indebted to Dr D.M. Lang's introduction to the translation of *Barlaam and Ioasaph* in the Loeb Classical Library edition 1967 (Volume entitled *St.John Damascene*), Heinemann and Harvard University Press.
6. See below, Part Two, ch.ii.
7. Ref. *Jewish Encyclopaedia* (Funk & Wagnalls) under *AEsop's Fables among the Jews* and *Barlaam and Josaphat*.
8. AEsop in *Herodotus*, Bk.Two, 134.
9. See above Part One, ch.viii, p.54.


CHAPTER TWO

1. *Balauhar and Budasaf*, pp.285-6. Quoted with references by Shaikh Abdul Qadir in his paper *Jesus Travels to India and Kashmir* published in the symposium *Truth about the Crucifixion* (read at the Inter. Conference on Deliverance of Jesus from the Cross, London 1978.)
2. Joseph Jacobs, *Barlaam and Josaphat*, 1896.
3. First printed in Iran in 1782 A.D. by Aga Mir Baqar at the Syed-us-Sanad press, quoted by Al-Haj Khwaja Nazir Ahmad in *Jesus in Heaven on Earth*, Lahore, 1972.
4. As we shall see in chapter vii below certain oriental writers go to quite extraordinary lengths to establish this identity.
5. *Khadim* means a caretaker. For the document here translated and passages from a number of other oriental texts which are quoted I am particularly indebted to the book *Jesus in Heaven on Earth*, by Al-Haj Khwaja Nazir Ahmad, fifth edition, Lahore, 1972.
6. See below p.108.
7. See above p.34.
8. The inference is understandable where there was no familiarity with Essene matters.
9. The MS. (No.189) is in the Library of the Royal Asiatic Society of Bengal.
10. *Hashmat-i-Kashmir*. MS. (No.42)in the Library of the Royal Asiatic Society of Bengal.
11. The original MS. is in the Buhar Library at Calcutta (No.81). A printed edition was made at Lahore in 1884.
12. Dr Lang, in the Introduction to the Loeb Classical Library edition of St.John Damascene: *Barlaam and Iosaph*, says that in the Roman Catholic Church these saints had their feast day on November 27. In the Greek Church Ioasaph's feast day was August 26, while the Russians commemorated not only the two saints, but the latter's father King Abenner, on November 19 (December 2 Old Style).


CHAPTER THREE

1. The English rendering of the extract quoted is that given by Al-Haj Khwaja Nazir Ahmad in his *Jesus in Heaven on Earth*, p.369.
2. Our authority states that Wien is a place of sulphur springs, about ten miles north-east of Srinagar.

3. *Mishnah, Megillah* iv.8–9. And see *Rev*.iii.4, vi.11, and vii.9.
4. Above p.102.
5. Above p.46.
6. The book was written in 1899. The English translation was made by Qazi Abdul Hamid, and first published in book form in 1944. The present edition, published by the London Mosque in 1978, has a valuable appendix of quotations.
7. See below ch.iv.
8. In the New Testament the *Epistle of James* is addressed to "the twelve tribes (of Israel) scattered abroad" and therefore reachable in terms of the Jewish Diaspora.
9. See above p.98.
10. See above p.101.
11. For the sources, see *Jesus in India* by Hazrat Mirza Ghulam Adhmad of Qadian, a work to which we have referred.
12. The reader is referred back to Part One, chs.ix and xi.

### CHAPTER FOUR

1. See *Jesus in India*, pp.53–54.
2. Dr Filip's paper was entitled *New View-points on Jesus's Activity Beyond Palestine*, and appeared on pp.170–171 of *Truth about the Crucifixion*, published by the London Mosque.
3. See above p.48.
4. *The Odes and Psalms of Solomon (2nd ed.)*: Cambridge University Press (1911).
5. See the *Clementine Homilies* and *Recognitions*.
6. Above p.46.
7. See Part Two, ch.iii.
8. See Part Two, ch.i.
9. See Part One, ch.vii.

### CHAPTER FIVE

1. *Isa*.ix.6–7. It was in the character of a Davidic Messiah that sonship of God was claimed for Jesus (*Mt*.xvi.16, *Jn*.i.49).
2. *The Sibylline Oracles*, Bk.iii.653–659 (tr.H.N.Bate).
3. Josephus, *Antiquities*, Bk.viii.185–186 (tr.Ralph Marcus). Loeb Classical Library.
4. Josephus, *Jewish War*, Bk.ii.128.
5. *Letter of Pliny to Trajan*.
6. *Eph*.v.14.
7. *Mt*.vi.29.
8. *Ezek*.sliv.15–17.
9. See above, p.73.
10. Above p.109.
11. G.T.Vigne, *Travels in Kashmir*, 1.395.
12. Dr James Ferguson, *Indian and Eastern Architecture*, p.286.
13. See above Part Two, ch.ii.

### CHAPTER SIX

1. See above Part Two, ch.iii.
2. For more detail see Schonfield, *The Passover Plot* and *After the Cross*.
3. See *Jesus in India*, ch.iii.
4. At least so far as present information serves. For details of the evidences on the scientific side the reader is referred to H.David Sox, *The Image on the Shroud* (Mandala Books, Unwin Paperbacks).

5. The legends that Jesus travelled to the Far East to evangelise the Lost Ten Tribes have already been shown to be groundless in a factual sense.


CHAPTER SEVEN

1. See Part Two, ch.ii, and also above p.95 on the relics of St. Josaphat.
2. In the *Indian Antiquity*. vol.299.
3. See above, p.98.
4. Above, p.98.
5. *Acts of Thomas*, 170.
6. Rendel Harris, *The Twelve Apostles* (Heffer, 1927), where the sources are cited.
7. See Part Two, ch.iv.
8. Above p.38. And of course, among the Apostles, Judas Iscariot might be described as a collector of alms.
9. *Acts of Thomas*, 163, and cp.*Rev*.iii.12.
10. Rendel Harris, *The Twelve Apostles*, p.40, citing G.M. Rae, *The Syrian Church in India*.
11. Capt.E.W.Wilfred, *Christian Religion in India*, p.70.
12. Rendel Harris, *The Twelve Apostles*, p.105.
13. Al-Haj Khwaja Nazir Ahmad, *Jesus in Heaven on Earth*, pp.358-359.
14. *Jesus in Heaven on Earth*, quoting Faqir Muhammad, *Jami-ul Tawarikh*, Vol.II, p.81.
15. See above, Part One, ch.viii.
16. *Against Apion*, i.26.
17. For the Essenes both Moses and the True Teacher were 'The Lawgiver'.
18. Schonfield, *Those Incredible Christians*, p.18. Iao or Io Sabaoth was the Greek equivalent of the Hebrew for the Lord of Hosts used by the Gnostics.


CHAPTER EIGHT

1. In *Tobit* in the Biblical Apocrypha the hero claims to be of the tribe of Napthali, and in *Lk*.ii.36 the prophetess Anna at Jerusalem is of the tribe of Asher. Nominally, both these tribes were 'lost'. Of course, there were the legends of the Lost Tribes beyond the River Sambatyon.
2. So the Mandaean *Haran Gawaita*. The number should perhaps be 6,000.
3. In article *Mandaean Polemic*, Bulletin of the School of Oriental and African Studies, Vol.xxv, Part 3, 1962.
4. Schonfield, *The Pentecost Revolution* (In U.S. *The Jesus Party*), p.28.
5. *Clementine Recognitions*, Bk.I, ch.lxxi.
6. See above, Part One, ch.xi.
7. Mingana, *The Early Spread of Christianity in Central Asia and the Far East: A New Document*, p.5-6 (Manchester: The University Press, and Longmans, Green & Co).
8. *Ibid.*, p.12.
9. *Ibid.*, p.16.
10. See above, p.104.
11. O.M.Burke, *Among the Dervishes* (Dutton & Co., New York).


CHAPTER NINE

1. See Schonfield, *The Jew of Tarsus*, ch.vii; *The Passover Plot*, Part 2 ch.iii; *Those Incredible Christians*, Supplementary Study 1, The Christology of Paul.
2. G. Vermes, *The Dead Sea Scrolls in English*, p.242.

3. *Ibid*.p.50.

4. *Gen*.i.26.

5. Cp.*Rev*.i.13–16, *Mk*.ix.2–3, also *Rev*.xix.11–16.

6. *Book of Enoch*, the *Similitudes*, xlvi.1–5, xlviii.1–10, lxii.2–16 (Tr.Charles).

7. See *Mk*.viii.38, xiii.26, xiv.62; *Mt*.xiii.41–42, xvi.27, xix.28, xxv.28, xxv.31–32; *Jn*.v.27; and see below Part Two, ch.xi.

8. Cp.*Isa*.ix.6–7.

9. *Hymns*, III.4 *(The Dead Sea Scrolls in English,* p.157).

10. See above, Part One, ch.ix, p.50. It is not unlikely that the story of the visit of the Magi in *Matthew* was borrowed from the Baptist cycle of legend.

11. The quotations are from the translation by G.R.S.Mead, *The Gnostic Baptizer* (J.M.Watkins, 1924).

12. *The Sibylline Oracles*, Bks III–v (Tr.H.N.Bate) in Translations of Early Documents: Series II, Hellenistic-Jewish Texts, S.P.C.K., 1918.

13. See above, Part Two, ch.v, and below ch.xii.

14. Virgil, *Eclogue* IV.4–10. (Tr.H.Rushton Fairclough), *Virgil* in the Loeb Classical Library, edition 1925.

CHAPTER TEN

1. Philo Judaeus, *On the Creation,* VIII. (Tr.Colson and Whitaker) Loeb Classical Library.

2. Philo, *On the Creation*,XXVIII.

3. Philo, *The Confusion of Tongues*,XXIII.

4. See below, ch.xi.

5. Philo, *On Flight and Founding*,XX.

6. See next chapter on the *Epistle to the Hebrews*.

7. *Mishnah*, *Chagigah*, ii.

8. Gershom G.Scholem, *Major Trends in Jewish Mysticism* (Thames and Hudson,1955).

9. See Frontispiece.

10. Epiphanius, *Panarion*, xxx.

11. Quoted above, p.139–140.

12. *Talmud Babli*, *Chagigah*, fol.12a. (Tr.A.W.Streane), Cambridge Univ. Press. According to *Genesis* (vi.1–4) when the Sons of God cohabited with the Daughters of Men inevitably their offspring were giants.

13. *Acts of John*, 90. (Tr.M.R.James), *The Apocryphal New Testament*, Oxford at the Clarendon Press.

CHAPTER ELEVEN

1. See above p.144.

2. *Genesis Rabba*, viii.1.

3. *Col*.i.15–19.

4. *Phil*.ii.5–11.

5. *Similitudes of Enoch*, xlviii.3–7 (Tr.Charles).

6. *Eph*.iv.12–13. The words italicised are for emphasis. The whole chapter in *Ephesians*, with parallels, should be consulted.

7. One of the Dead Sea Scrolls was on this theme. And see *Eph*.v.5–8; *1.Thess*.v.5.

8. *Heb*.ii.14–18.

9. *Heb*.vii.4–10. See also above Part One, ch.vi.

CHAPTER TWELVE

1. J.M.Robertson, *Pagan Christs*, pp.315–316.

2. Justin, *I.Apol.* ch.66.
3. Tertullian, *Praescr.* ch.40.
4. Josephus, *Jewish War,* II.128-9.
5. See above, p.118.
6. Part Two, ch.v.
7. See Gershom Scholem, *Major Trends in Jewish Mysticism,* p.67f (Thames and Hudson, 1955), and *Jewish Encyclopaedia,* Article *Metatron.*
8. *Ibid.* p.70. See also under 'Metatron' *The Religion and Worship of the Synagogue,* Oesterley & Box.
9. Oesterley and Box, *op.cit.,* p.175.
10. *Sanhed.,* 39b.
11. *Talmud Babli, Chagigah,* 15a.
12. Cp.*Rev.*xxii.20, "Even so, come, Lord Jesus."
13. "The ten directions".Cp. the invisible lines in different direction which link the *Sefiroth,* portrayed in the Frontispiece.
14. See Edward Conze, *Buddhist Scriptures,* pp.238-240 (Penguin Books, 1959).
15. See above, Part Two, ch.x, especially pp. 144-145.

### CHAPTER THIRTEEN

1. Lk.xvii.20-21 (Tr.Hugh Schonfield), *The Authentic New Testament.*
2. *Thanksgiving Psalms,* 19, according to the listing and translation of G. Vermes, *The Dead Sea Scrolls in English* (Pelican Books, 1962).

### APPENDIX A

1. *HBHG,* p.37.
2. *HBHG,* p.42.
3. *HBHG,* p.45.
4. *HBHG.* p.47.
5. See Frontispiece to this volume.
6. *HBHG,* p.54, quoting Oursel, *Le Procès des Templiers,* p.208.
7. See R.M. Grant, *Gnosticism and Early Christianity* (Oxford University Press; in U.S. Columbia University Press, 1959).
8. Grant, *op.cit.* p.77.
9. Plutarch, *Of Isis and Osiris,* 3.
10. Grant, *op.cit.* p.84.
11. *HBHG,* plate 16b.

# Bibliography

## PART ONE

### ANCIENT EXTRA-BIBLICAL SOURCES EMPLOYED

The Apocrypha, Books of *Maccabees, Ecclesiasticus*: Pseudepigrapha, *Assumption of Moses, Testaments of the IXX Patriarchs*, Book of *Jubilees, Ascension of Isaiah, Psalms of Solomon, Odes of Solomon*: Uncanonical Gospels, *Gospel of the hebrews, Gospel of Thomas*: The Dead Sea Scrolls, *Damascus Document, habbakuk Commentary, The Community Rule, Thanksgiving Psalms, War of the Sons of Light with the Sons of Darkness: Targum of Palestine*: Talmud and Midrash, Mishnah *Aboth*, Mishnah *Chagigah*, Mishnah *Sanhedrin*; Talmud *Shabbath, Baba Metsiah, Taanith, Sanhedrin, Aboda Zara*; Midrash, *Tehillim, Pirke de R. Eliezer, Genesis Rabba*: Josephus, *Jewish War, Antiquities of the Jews, Against Apion*: Philo, *On the Contemplative Life*: Patristic Literature, *Didache; Teaching of the XII Apostles, Apostolic Constitutions*; Hippolytus of Rome, *Commentary on the Blessings of Isaac, Jacob and Moses*; Ephraim the Syrian, *Gospel Commentaries;* Origen, *Against Celsus*; Eusebius, *Ecclesiastical History*; Hegessippus, *Memoirs;* Clementine *Homilies; Epistle of Clement to James;* Epiphanius, *Panarion; Refutation of All Heresies: Biblical Antiquities of Philo: Seder Olam: Sefer Refuot*: Mandaean *Sidra d'Yahya: Barlaam and Joasaph*: Pliny, *Natural History*.

### MODERN AUTHORITIES EMPLOYED

Rappoport, *Myths and Legends of Ancient Israel*: G. Vermes, *The Dead Sea Scrolls in English*: J. Teicher in *Journal of Jewish Studies*, Vol. 2: Jewish Encyclopaedia (Funk & Wagnalls), Articles *Asaph ben Berechiah* and *Joseph*: Dupont-Sommer, *The Jewish Sect of Qumran and the Essenes*: Moses Gaster, *Samaritan Eschatology*: J. M. Allegro, *The Dead Sea Scrolls*: M. Baigent, R. Leigh and H. Lincoln, *The Holy Blood and the Holy Grail*: Schonfield, *Secrets of the Dead Sea Scrolls, According to the Hebrews, Saints Against Caesar*: A. Mingana, *Life of John the Baptist by Serapion* (Bulletin of the John Rylands Library, July 1927): Robert Eisler, *The Messiah Jesus and John the Baptist*: A. Mingana, *Some Judaeo-Christian Documents in the John Rylands Library*: Shlomo Pines, *The Jewish Christians of the Early Centuries of Christianity according to a New Source* (Israel Academy of Sciences and Humanities, Vol. 2), *The Oath of Asaph the Physician and Yohanan ben Zabda* (Israel Academy of Sciences and Humanities, Vol. 5): McNeile, Journal of Biblical Literature, Vol. 12): E. S. Drower, *Mandaean Polemic* (Bulletin of the School of Oriental and African Studies, Vol. 25): R. H. Charles, *Fragments of a Zadokite Work*: R. T. Herford, *Christianity in Talmud and Midrash*: J. Parkes, The Conflict of the Church and the Synagogue: S. Schechter, *Documents of Jewish Sectaries*,

Macuch, *Alter und Heimat der Mandäismus nach neuerscholssenen Quellen*: H. Gregoire, *Les Gens de la Caverne, les Qaraites et les Khazars (Le Flambeau,* Brussels 1952).

## PART TWO

### CHAPTER ONE

Robert Eisler, *The Messiah Jesus and John the Baptist* (Methuen, 1931).

D. M. Lang, *Barlaam and Joasaph* in *St. John Damascene* (Loeb Classical Library, Heineman and Harvard Univ. Press).

Jewish Encyclopaedia (Funk & Wagnalls), articles *AEsop's Fables among the Jews* and *Barlaam & Josaphat*.

### CHAPTER TWO

Shaikh Al-Said-us-Sadiq, *Kamal-ud-Din*.

Joseph Jacobs, *Barlaam and Josaphat*, 1896.

Kwaja Nazir Ahmad, *Jesus in Heaven and on Earth* (Lahore, 1972).

Mullah Nadiri, *Tarikh-i-Kashmir*.

H. H. Cole, *Illustrations of Ancient Buildings in Kashmir* (London, 1869).

Abdul Qadir, *Jesus Travels to India and Kashmir*, in the Symposium *Truth about the Crucifixion* (London Mosque, 1978).

### CHAPTER THREE

J. P. Ferrier, *History of the Afghans,* 1858.

Hazrat Mirza Ghulam Ahmad, *Masih Hindustani Mein*, 1899, tr. by Qazi Abdul Hamid as *Jesus in India,* 1944, and reprinted by the London Mosque, 1978.

### CHAPTER FOUR

Roger de Wendover, *Flores Historiarum*, 1228.

Ladislav Filip, *New Viewpoints on Jesus's Activity Beyond Palestine*, published in *Truth about the Crucifixion* (London Mosque, 1978).

### CHAPTER FIVE

G. T. Vigne, *Travels in Kashmir*.

James Ferguson, *India and Eastern Architecture*.

### CHAPTER SIX

H. J. Schonfield, *The Passover Plot* (Hutchinson, 1965). In Paperback Bantam Books.

H. J. Schonfield, *After the Cross* (A. S. Barnes, 1981).

### CHAPTER SEVEN

Rendel Harris, *The Twelve Apostles* (Heffer, 1927).

E. W. Wilfred, *Christian Religion in India*.

H. J. Schonfield, *Those Incredible Christians* (Hutchinson, 1968).

### CHAPTER EIGHT

Thomson, *The Land and the Book*.

S. Drower, *Mandaean Polemic* (Bulletin of the School of Oriental and African Studies, Vol. xxv, Part 3, 1962).
H. J. Schonfield, *The Pentecost Revolution* (Macdonald, 1974). Published in U.S.A. as *The Jesus Party* (Macmillan, New York).
A. Mingana, *The Early Spread of Christianity in Central Asia and the Far East: A New Document* (Manchester: The University Press and Longmans, Green & Co.).
O. M. Burke, *Among the Dervishes* (Dutton, New York).

CHAPTER NINE

H. J. Schonfield, *The Jew of Tarsus* (Macdonald).
G. Vermes, *The Dead Sea Scrolls in English* (Pelican Books, 1962).
G. R. S. Mead, *The Gnostic Baptizer* (Watkins, 1924).
T. W. Bate, *The Sibylline Oracles: Books 3-5* (SPCK, 1918).
H. Rushton Fairclough, *Virgil* (Loeb Classical Library, 1925).

CHAPTER TEN

Colson & Whitaker, *Philo Judaeus* (Heinemann & Harvard Univ. Press, 1962).
G. Scholem, *Major Trends in Jewish Mysticism* (Thames & Hudson, 1955).
A. W. Streane, *Talmud Babli: Chagigah* (Cambridge Univ. Press, 1891).
M. R. James, *The Apocryphal New Testament* (Oxford, the Clarendon Press, 1926).

CHAPTER TWELVE

J. M. Robertson, *Pagan Christs* (Watts, 1903).
Oesterley and Box, *The Religion and Worship of the Synagogue* (Pitman, 1907).
Edward Conze, *Buddhist Scriptures* (Penguin 1959).
H. J. Schonfield, *The Authentic New Testament* (Dobson, 1956).

APPENDIX A

Baigent, Leighton & Lincoln, *The Holy Blood & The Holy Grail* (Cape, 1983).
R. M. Grant, *Gnosticism and Early Christianity* (OUP & Columbia Univ. Press, 1959).